Principles of Export Guidebooks

Series Editor: Michael Z. Brooke

Principles of International Trade and Payments

Peter Briggs

Learning Resources
Centre

First published 1994
Reprinted 1995, 1997

Blackwell Publishers Ltd
108 Cowley Road
Oxford OX4 1JF, UK

Blackwell Publishers Inc
350 Main Street
Malden, Massachusetts 02148, USA

British Library Cataloguing in Publication Data
A CIP catalogue record for this book is available from the British Library

Library of Congress Cataloging in Publication Data
Briggs, Peter D.
Principles of international trade and payments / Peter D. Briggs
p. cm.—(Principles of export guidebooks)
Includes index.
ISBN 0–631–19163–1
1. International trade. 2. Export credit. 3. International finance.
I. Title. II. Series: Principles of export guide books.
HF1379.B75   1995   94–15853
382—dc20   CIP

Typeset in 11.5 on 13.5pt Garamond Light
by Aitch Em Wordservice, Aylesbury, Buckinghamshire, Great Britain
Printed and bound in Great Britain by Hartnolls Ltd, Bodmin, Cornwall

This book is printed on acid-free paper

Contents

List of Figures and Exhibits

Foreword

This book on International Trade and Payments is the third in our series of export texts.

Peter Briggs, the author, is a well-known adviser on export issues and brings a wealth of experience to bear on the subject in this well written book.

It is thoroughly recommended to all who are making a career in exporting.

The Earl of Limerick, President,
The Institute of Export

Series Editor's Introduction

In launching the third of this series of guidebooks to the profession of exporting, the series editor – along with others associated with the project – is pleased to welcome Peter Briggs as its author.

Like the book on legal issues, *Principles of International Trade and Payments* is necessarily more technical than some in the series. The author's contribution to the development of you, the reader, rests on his long experience as a trade finance consultant and I present this book with great pride to the exporting public.

There is another book in this series (*Principles of Physical Distribution*) which covers some of the same ground but in a different way; all the books are preoccupied with bringing products to foreign markets (what else is export about?) and this volume focuses on the essential aim of any exporter – obtaining payment by as secure and speedy a method as possible.

May I welcome you, the reader, and hope to meet you again as the other books in the series appear on all aspects of export which you need to know – law (for the non-lawyer), transport and distribution, international marketing, market research, and export management in addition to the first book in the series which is a review of the whole subject.

Michael Z. Brooke

About The Institute of Export Examinations

The Institute is grateful for the initiative of Michael Z. Brooke, the series editor, and Blackwell Publishers in publishing this unique series of books specially written for the Professional Examinations.

The authors for the series have been carefully selected and have specialized knowledge of their subjects, all being established lecturers or examiners for the Professional Examinations.

The books have been written in a style that is of benefit not only to students of The Institute but also to commercial organizations seeking further information about specific aspects of international trade.

Professionalism in export is vital for every company if they are to compete successfully in world markets and this new series of books provides a sound basis of knowledge for all those seeking a professional qualification in export through The Institute of Export's Professional Examinations.

The book covers the following parts of The Institute's syllabus.

International Trade and Payments

Objectives of the Syllabus

1 To describe the framework within which international trade is conducted.

2 To describe the terms and conditions on which trade is conducted.
3 To consider the means of financing export trade and their application.

General survey of international trade

1 Commodity markets – merchants, brokers, futures, etc.
2 Multinational companies – advantages and disadvantages.
3 Economic, commercial and political factors.
4 Balance of Payments including Balance of Trade.
5 Invisibles and capital movements.
6 Outline of international, financial and trade organizations, e.g. IMF, IBRD, GATT, EBRD.
7 Countertrade – barter, counterpurchase, buy-back, offset, switch trading, evidence accounts.
8 Trading with Eastern Europe.
9 Trading within the European Community.

Export prices and terms of sale

1 Quoting ex works to DDP build up of retail price, including packing, transport, insurance, duties, etc.
2 Agents' commission and/or distributors' mark ups.
3 Sales terms offered – open account, cash with order, cash against documents, Bills of Exchange D/P or D/A.
4 Documentary credits.
5 Credit management – status enquiries, fixing limits.

Foreign exchange

1 Quoting prices in buyers' currency.
2 Exchange risk – use of Forward Exchange market to eliminate risk – borrowing the foreign currency.

Collection of payment

1 Credit risk cover and transfer risk – Export Credit Insurance.
2 Degrees of risk according to terms of sale.
3 Open account sales – payment to be remitted by buyer – by mail transfer, telegraphic transfer, SWIFT, etc.
4 Bills of Exchange – collection procedure through exporter's bank (remitting) and overseas bank (collecting).
5 Uniform Rules for Collections – Protesting, Case of Need, etc.
6 Documentary credits.
7 Use of Export Houses – Sales to Export Merchants – sales through Confirming Houses.
8 Pick-a-back schemes. Group selling.
9 Factoring companies – administer sales ledger and collect payments.

Documentary credits

1 Irrevocable and revocable.
2 Confirmed and unconfirmed.
3 Transferable and back-to-back credits.
4 Revolving credits.
5 Acceptance credit facility – often from Acceptance Houses and linked to Documentary collections.
6 Red Clause credit.

Sources of bank finance

1 Negotiation of Bills of Exchange (Discount or Purchase).
2 Loans against collections outstanding – pledge by Letter of Hypothecation.
3 Banks' smaller (up to £1 million) and larger (over £1 million) Export Schemes – credit period 180 days (which may be extended) – by arrangement with Export Credit Insurance Companies. Banks provide non-recourse finance of up to 90% of invoice value for exporters who hold a credit insurance policy.

4 Banks smaller and larger Export Schemes as above but the Exporter is nominated as joint policyholder with bank.
5 Medium-term arrangement – bank provides post-shipment finance to exporter selling on credit terms of from two to five years from date of shipment against a specific unconditional guarantee from ECGD – finance at fixed rate.
6 Long-term finance – buyer finance – ECGD guarantees loans to overseas buyer and so enables supplier to be paid in cash. This principle also applies to provide finance to say a State organization for a basket of purchases.
7 Exporters selling on Open Account and using the services of a Factoring Company may also obtain advances from the Factor against outstanding debts.
8 Forfaiting – Forfaiter purchases Bills of Exchange without recourse drawn by exporter and accepted by overseas buyer which usually bears the aval or unconditional guarantee of buyer's bank.

Other trading methods

1 Consignment Trading.
2 Joint Ventures.
3 Royalty agreements.
4 Licensing.

Bank finance for imports

1 Security in the Documents of Title of the goods. Pledge to bank and subsequent release on Trust if required to effect sale.

Other documents of interest

1 Indemnities – to shipping company in case of absence of Bills of Lading or to bank to cover discrepancies in documents presented.
2 Bonds – Tender, Performance and Advance Payment. Situations

in which used – issued by UK Bank or its Correspondent in Buyer's Country – Types, On Demand and Conditional – Expiry dates and extensions – Unfair Calling.

R.T. Ebers FIEx,
Director of Education & Training,
The Institute of Export

Preface

During the years following the Second World War national leaders have variously described the export industry as a patriotic duty, a challenge and, in the best remembered comment, as fun. While the experienced exporter endeavouring to supply goods over barely adequate roads to an impoverished African country might smile wryly at the last description, the common factor to all these comments is that they were made in the knowledge that export is vital to the United Kingdom economy and our industrial and commercial sectors must be encouraged to exploit opportunities for selling abroad.

Of all the economic activities it is difficult to imagine one more relevant to our everyday lives than exporting. Without it we would be unable to earn the foreign exchange necessary to defray the costs of imports we require not only to supply raw materials, of which we have no indigenous source of supply or insufficient to provide the needs of industry, but also to enable us to enjoy a wide variety of consumer goods and commodities from abroad without which our standard of living would be severely prejudiced. The flexibility which exports provide to industry by ensuring a variety of markets, some perhaps in deep recession while others are not so adversely affected, is a source of strength and profitability. That same flexibility may also help to lessen the debilitating effects of recession-based unemployment since while, on occasion, recession can be worldwide, at other times export demand from some markets may reduce the

redundancies which might otherwise arise from stagnation or falling sales in the domestic or other markets.

The success or failure of our export industry, being the main contributor to the current account statement in our balance of payments, will also have a direct effect on fiscal policy as determined in the Chancellor's annual Budget and thus indirectly on the taxation to which we may be subject, and the interest rates which determine our ability to borrow, including the emotive subject of mortgages.

The exporter is thus carrying a responsibility not only for the success or otherwise of his or her own business but, in a real sense, for the well-being of the United Kingdom and the quality of living of its peoples. A nation is no more able than a company or individual to live beyond its means and to endeavour to do so can only result in the painful constraints and belt tightening which we, in common with other offenders, have suffered from time to time.

Success in exporting, as with many other activities, is much more likely to be achieved by the professional and not an amateur approach. Exhortations to export made in the past have not always been accompanied by the stress on professionalism required and the determination to make more widely available the assistance necessary to achieve that end. It has somehow been assumed that, as in the Olympic Games, the importance of exporting lies as much in the taking part as in succeeding. Alas, the contribution of the exporter whose sales are not carried through to the obtaining of payment cannot be described as other than negative.

Professionalism is attained by a combination of skills applied to different aspects of exporting. Other books in this series deal with a variety of such skills, and this volume with the essential aim of any exporter; obtaining payment by as secure and speedy a method as possible. We shall look briefly at the history of international trade and any lessons it may have for us and the structure or environment in which a would-be exporter has to operate; what we might perhaps describe as the rules of the game. Thereafter we follow the exporter's progress through the many financial pitfalls which may line the road to a successfully completed overseas sale and the receipt of settlement;

examining the individual risks and the ways in which they may be eliminated or minimized by the true professional.

To assist the student there is included at the end of this book a series of self testing questions, chapter by chapter, which will reveal if the salient facts have been understood. Additionally, that list is followed by one identifying, where appropriate, topics which could usefully provide the basis for company seminars seeking to apply the general principles to the specific circumstances of the company. The Institute of Export is able, upon request, to provide experts who can assist company executives in organizing and conducting such seminars.

Acknowledgements

SITPRO Exhibit 6.3 is reproduced by kind permission of BBA and SITPRO.

ICC United Kingdom For their ready co-operation in allowing the inclusion of numerous references to ICC Publications.

Lloyds Bank Acknowledgements and Disclaimers are shown in the exhibits in chapters 5 and 6.

Paul Barnett Manager of Lloyds Bank Plc South West Regional International Branch Southampton, whose advice on current banking practice in relation to international trading customers has been extremely valuable and whose sympathetic understanding of an exporter's financial problems I found very encouraging.

Finally to **my wife Fay** for her willing acceptance of the loss of my company for so many hours and to **Eveline** for her help in the preparation of the text.

1

The Rules of the Game

The beginning of international trade is sufficiently ancient to
defy exact determination but it was certainly well-established
in biblical times. The commencement of trade as we know it
today probably occurred in Tudor times with the emergence of
thrustful merchants, particularly in England, Spain and Portugal.
If the date of the first international deal is uncertain, the reasons
for its taking place are not difficult to imagine. As travel increased, often as a result of wars or incursions into neighbouring
countries, the knowledge of desirable goods available beyond
the boundaries of one's home country expanded and demand
was created. No doubt also the early traders realized that a good
living could be made from satisfying that demand. The knowledge brought with it a realization that few, if any, countries are
wholly self sufficient.

The Law of Comparative Costs

In addition to the wish to import goods which they could not
produce themselves, perhaps due to climatic conditions or an
uneven distribution worldwide of natural resources, nations
realized that some goods could not be produced at home in
sufficient quantities to meet internal demand and others were
more cheaply produced abroad. This last realization came to be
recognized in the law of comparative costs which is essential to

the understanding of national specialization and the principles underlying international trade. The law states that a country should concentrate on those products (including commodities, raw materials and manufactures) which it can produce at the maximum cost advantage in comparison with other countries, and trade those for products in respect of which other countries have the comparative cost advantage in production. The following simple example illustrates the law.

Countries A and B each have ten production capability units of equal value, five of them are devoted to producing barley and five to producing sugar beet.

With its units country A produces 50 measures of barley and 20 measures of sugar beet.

Country B with its units produces 30 measures of barley and 40 measures of sugar beet.

Clearly country A is a more efficient producer of barley than is country B but conversely country B produces sugar beet more efficiently than does country A.

Applying the law of comparative costs to the example let us assume country A devotes all of its ten production capability units to producing barley, while country B concentrates its ten units on producing sugar beet; the results are:

country A produces 100 measures of barley;
country B produces 80 measures of sugar beet.

Thus, by specializing within each country on the production of the commodity in which it has a comparative cost advantage, the overall production of both commodities in the two countries is increased. Provided demand exists for the increased production it is clear that for each to concentrate in this way is to their mutual advantage and enables trade in barley from country A to country B, and in sugar beet from country B to country A.

Certain factors may distort the application of the law of comparative costs in our modern world (for example: transport costs, duties, tariffs and quotas) and in some instances countries may seek domestic production deliberately even though this is more costly than importing, the classic example being national interest products such as armaments. Nevertheless the law is basically as true today as when it was originally propounded.

How Did International Trade Begin?

International trade in the beginning was on a barter basis, commodities and raw materials being exchanged for each other and for the limited number of manufactured goods available. However as volumes increased a medium of exchange had to be found. To ensure universal acceptance of money (the medium widely adopted) coins were of precious metals, usually gold or silver, and the exchange of coins, which was the forerunner of modern day foreign exchange dealing, was already taking place in Roman times. It was upon this early development that the acceleration of trade was made possible as travel opened up new opportunities. Today we have the traditional pattern of industrialized countries supplying manufactures against raw materials and commodities, supplemented by a wide measure of specialization within manufactured goods themselves giving rise to increased trade opportunities.

The Benefits of International Trade

In summary, the benefits from developing international trade are that it provides a wide selection of goods in the market place which, because they are produced where costs are lowest, are at the most competitive price to the consumer. Producers also benefit from the economies in cost resulting from supplying a wider market than that obtainable within their own country. As goods traded internationally may pass through a chain of buyers and sellers and require the assistance of various service industries, carriers, forwarders, insurers and banks among others, the overall increase in trade is magnified.

The Structure of International Trade

The structure of international trade is more complex than it might appear at first sight. Because the concept is the most familiar face of exporting, we are often unaware that direct export is not the only form of international trading. The method of selling, buying or in some cases exchanging goods between countries differs according to the goods and market concerned. The structure, which should not be confused with the varying channels for distribution of goods (a subject covered in a companion book in this series) comprises direct exporting, countertrade, commodity trading, multinational operations, subsidiaries and joint ventures.

Direct exporting

Direct exporting is the shipment of goods by the seller to either an agent or distributor, who on-sells the products to the end buyer, or direct to that buyer, payment being made by the agent, distributor or buyer directly or through the banking system. It accounts for a very substantial part of international trade and is almost invariably the method adopted by the new exporter. For established exporters, with the exception of large national and multinational firms, direct exporting is also normal where manufactured goods and developed markets are involved.

Commodity markets

Today considerable international trade consists of the sale by industrialized countries of manufactured goods to what we term Lesser Developed Countries (LDCs). While these sales are normally effected by direct export, the sales of the commodities and raw materials by the country from which the necessary foreign exchange for payment is derived are usually accomplished by a different method.

Commodities in this context may be defined as primary products, for example, wheat, coffee, jute and raw materials which are marketed internationally either in their original state or after conversion into a form acceptable to the market such as metal ingots. Traditionally producers of commodities, many of them in the less developed countries, have rarely had direct contact with importers in the countries where ultimate buyers reside. This may result in some cases from a lack of sophistication in the selling country but in many instances it arises from the fact that many producers have relatively small operations. Thus in Australia there are numerous wool producers but they collectively supply the markets through merchants trading in the Sydney auctions. This system, which has its counterpart in many other commodities, is not a sign of an uninformed approach to markets; quite the reverse. Merchants can grade products in order to provide for the market's needs and by dealing with multiple buyers can become receptive to changes in demand of which an individual producer might well remain unaware.

Commodity markets exist in many countries and, for historical reasons, London is one of the most important. Within the market, which is basically a device for channelling commodities from producers or merchants to manufacturers, wholesalers or other principal buyers, sellers' representatives or merchants are able to deal with buyers, striking a price through brokers.

There are a number of types of commodity market and while all are characterized by the broker members dealing between themselves on the market floor and thereby acting as intermediaries between producers and buyers, the method by which buyers are able to satisfy themselves that the merchandise is to their requirements differs. In certain markets, for example fruit and vegetables, the produce is offered in specific lots which a buyer is able to inspect before purchase and he will take physical delivery immediately the transaction is completed.

Others, such as tea, provide the potential purchaser with the opportunity to taste samples taken from stocks held in bonded warehouses and made available to the market by the selling brokers. If satisfied with the quality the buyer will complete the deal receiving the quantity ordered from the stock which has provided the sample tasting.

A third type of market of which The London Metal Exchange is typical, operates entirely through specification. Neither the buyer nor the members of the market will see the actual consignment of say tin, lead or copper which is being bought and sold but will have before them the exact specification which is required. These specifications have worldwide recognition and are sufficiently detailed to ensure that the chance of an unsatisfactory delivery is minimal. It is indicative of the trust placed by buyers in the system that these markets have provided a competitive means of dealing in the commodities concerned for as long as London has been a recognized centre for trade.

Economic, Commercial and Political Factors

At this point in our survey of the rules of the game we must consider a difficult situation facing many exporters which has arisen during the last 40 years. When future historians look back to the period from the conclusion of World War II to the present day it must surely provide one of the most fascinating studies in world trade. Prior to the war the principles underlying the law of comparative costs could be readily seen in the overseas trading of the United Kingdom. This country's manufactured goods found a ready market in Commonwealth countries (and many others) and it bought from them raw materials and commodities, the trade being assisted by a system of reduced tariffs known as commonwealth preference.

The end of the war brought changes in the political and moral thinking of the world which were to have profound effects on trading patterns. The spread of communism into the countries of Eastern Europe and beyond had as great an influence on trade as politics; the fear that exposure to capitalist systems might have a corrupting effect led to the creation of COMECON, a trading bloc which paralleled the Warsaw Pact in military strategy. Not only did COMECON seek to stimulate internal trade, it positively discouraged trade relations with countries forming the outside world except when emergencies, such as chronic shortages of foodstuffs, compelled exceptions. Settlements for internal trade were made in national currencies, often not convertible in foreign exchange markets abroad, and

6

the amount of convertible currencies available for such trade as was conducted outside COMECON was minimal. The result was a large potential market taken from the normal trading of the West.

A further disruption to the pre-war pattern arose from a surge of emotion over the concept of empire. The fervent worldwide movement towards independence for individual nations, not always having considered their ability to survive as viable entities, exerted moral pressure on public and governments alike, leading inexorably to such independence being granted, if any approach demanded, and actively encouraged. An extension to this feeling was experienced by countries having a large proportion of their population without an effective voice in government and administration, the prime example among significant trading nations being South Africa. Trade became an instrument to be used in pressurising for political change and sanctions served to contract potential markets. Often countries gaining independence sought, as a matter of national pride, to reduce the trading ties with the former mother country, the continuance of which were somehow thought to imply a continued dependence. In other cases it found a supplier more favourably placed geographically who could offer keener prices. Even where the relationship remained unchanged – Australia, for example, remained a Commonwealth country – the ties were insufficient to warrant a continuance of trade at the same level if competitive influences favoured trading partners who were more conveniently positioned.

The background against which these changes have to be assessed is highly significant. The cost of war to both victor and vanquished was extremely heavy and the United Kingdom had invested vast sums in its war effort and found its resources greatly reduced. The natural reaction was to seek new markets, a desire strengthened by the commitment of its government to full employment as a political necessity for survival. If, as suggested by the law of comparative costs, new markets were to be sought where manufactures were in demand and raw materials and commodities were available for purchase this pinpointed the Third World or Lesser Developed Countries (LDCs), many of which were the newly independent nations, as priorities. This direction of thinking became even more pronounced as the years passed and the continental war-torn economies revived until eventually they also became competitors in the quest for new markets.

The problem of international debt

The Third World answered the criteria for marketing but its resources for payment, derived from the export of primary products, were insufficient to satisfy the industrialized nations' appetite for exports. In endeavouring to solve the dilemma by lending long term to Less Developed Countries, at first through government finance or guarantee backing and later by private sector loans to overseas governments representing a sovereign risk (which was then thought to be minimal), the ultimate disaster of the liquidity crisis was born.

It is always easy to be wise after the event and it must be recognized that the lending, although not always thought through in the long term, did not seem as imprudent at the time as it does today. The economies of most of the Less Developed Countries appeared reasonably healthy. Natural resources offered considerable potential, reputable financial institutions and indirectly, government, were supportive and the loan portfolios of lenders initially contained minimal exposure to Less Developed Countries. On risk-spread calculations lenders were enthusiastic, competing fiercely for the opportunity to lend at margins appreciably more attractive than those on domestic corporate lending. What then went wrong?

The borrowing which Less Developed Countries were encouraged to undertake was used to finance projects designed to improve infrastructure, an aim which was in itself commendable. However it must be added that some of the projects were ambitious and were based on assumptions which were not always proved correct.

An excellent example was the funds borrowed to exploit oil reserves where these existed in Less Developed Countries. At the time international oil prices were rising rapidly with threatened restriction on production by OPEC countries and reserves, which had with lower prices seemed uneconomic to develop, suddenly appeared viable and a potential source of assistance to those countries which were fortunate enough to possess them. Subsequently oil prices fell due to various reasons, including more efficient management of resources by users and OPEC's difficulty in persuading some members to limit production. The result was that many of the Less Developed Countries' schemes for exploitation became of doubtful viability.

The earnings of a number of countries also fell short of estimates at the time borrowings were contracted. Where the balance of payments depended on primary products being sold on world markets to provide the necessary income in foreign currency both to pay for imports and service borrowing, the price rises in those products proved far less than those for the manufactured goods imported. This problem was aggravated for Less Developed Countries which had no indigenous oil by the need to purchase at high prices during the height of the oil crisis, which had a greater effect on their economies than those of industrialized countries.

Much of the borrowing was on what we know as roll over terms; the interest margin varying each time the loan was extended for a further period. Interest rates rose significantly over the period and this again added to the servicing costs.

An interesting factor which also contributed to the crisis was the increase in democratization in a number of the Less Developed Countries. The result was that their governments experienced, often for the first time, the pressure of public opinion. Frequently that opinion contrasted the minimal rise in their living standards with the considerable portion of national income devoted to the servicing of foreign loans; this produced pressure to postpone repayments or even repudiate the debt. Rescheduling was the only temporary solution to these severe problems but, despite growing attempts to find a more permanent answer by both government and private sectors, huge provisions have been made by the lenders against bad debts.

Countertrade

The developments described both in Eastern Europe and the Less Developed Countries have meant that exporters to those areas have found it increasingly difficult to obtain payment and, in consequence, trade by conventional methods is very limited. The ingenious answer has been the rise of a new addition to the structure of international trade, namely countertrade.

Countertrade is, in many respects, a reversion to the age old practice of exchange of goods which existed before money was invented, but it enables money to be received ultimately through disposal of the goods countertraded. Indeed this is an apt comparison because countertrade is a method of trading normally, although not invariably, resorted to only if the prospect of straightforward payment is not a viable option.

There are five main categories of countertrade; barter, counterpurchase, off-set, buy-back, switch trading and evidence accounts, each designed to deal with a different set of circumstances. However all have a common principle, the sale of goods by an exporter who is tied contractually to a purchase or obligation to purchase goods from the buyer's country. New exporters and those who, while experienced, have not dealt with this type of transaction previously should be warned that countertrade is a highly complex subject and should only be undertaken after consultation with, and the assistance of, specialists in the field.

Among the pitfalls justifying this cautious approach perhaps the most important is that exporters are offered goods in respect of which they have no experience in trading. Such goods require expert assessment of their value and knowledge of any impediments to their import as regards regulations or quotas. The value of the goods countertraded is unlikely to equal exactly that of those exported and the timing of the sale and purchase seldom coincide, arrangements being required to bridge the gap. This may mean credit being given in circumstances where risk is considerable. To provide against loss in these unusual conditions the drawing up of contracts and arrangements for shipment require particular care.

Fortunately many specialists in countertrade exist in London and their specialization may reflect experience either in the goods offered to the exporter or in dealing with the country to which the export is being made. Although any exporter being offered business of this type should immediately seek expert advice (The Department of Trade and Industry will be able to advise on suitable sources) it is useful to appreciate the general characteristics of the five types of countertrade.

Barter

Barter is the category of countertrade most akin to the practices in the pre-monetary era. Goods are accepted directly in exchange for those exported, there being in theory no monetary settlement involved. However it is quite usual for the seller to delay shipment until all or part of the bartered goods have been sold. The essential feature which distinguishes this category is that a single contract covers both sale and purchase by the exporter.

Counterpurchase

Unlike barter, counterpurchase involves two independent but related contracts. The first covers the export from (say) the United Kingdom and has all the normal provisions regarding settlement on delivery or after an agreed credit period. The second covers the purchase, or intention to purchase, by the exporter of the agreed goods or services from the buyer's country which may be for a value representing up to 100 per cent or more of the first contract.

The flexibility reflected in these transactions as regards the nature of the goods counterpurchased, their destination and the arrangements made for their sale is very considerable but it is the principle of the agreement to counterpurchase as a condition of the original export order which is the vital factor. This form of countertrade has been very common particularly in Eastern European countries but is also present in trade with certain of the Lesser Developed Countries.

Offset

Offset is designed to reduce the net cost to a country of buying very expensive plants, systems or other goods and is frequently seen when the order is very large or of sensitive composition and likely to attract widespread publicity. For example in fields such as military and civil aircraft, radar systems and other military equipment, publicity focuses on the possible effects of substantial imports on the indigenous industry.

To counteract criticism it is agreed by the suppliers that they will incorporate into aircraft, systems or plant supplied, components originating within the importing country, thus offsetting the cost of the import and mitigating the effects of unemployment in the indigenous manufacturers who might otherwise have supplied the entire order. A similar effect is sometimes achieved by undertakings to manufacture certain components locally or to engage in cooperative ventures which use the advanced knowhow of the exporting country to the benefit of industries within the importing country.

Buy-back

Buy-back is most frequently seen where a country desires to purchase a complete plant from abroad, usually for the production of consumer goods. The cost may be utterly prohibitive when measured against foreign exchange available, and in the case of consumer orientated manufactures the international aid which is often available for infrastructural projects may not be on offer. In these instances the exporter may give to the importer assurances that payment will be accepted, in whole or in part, in the form of goods produced by the plant and bought back from the importing country under a contractual agreement.

The time scale implicit in such dealings, which accept that purchases of finished products cannot commence until the plant is in full operation, means that the sale of the plant is on very extended credit terms. This will of course be very attractive to the importing country but it should be added that, if the production of the finished product is achieved at a much reduced cost compared to that in the exporting country, it may also carry considerable advantages to the exporters. This category of countertrade was very popular with the former Soviet Union as it dovetailed well into long term economic planning.

Switch trading

As we have seen, exports to a market are normally paid for out of the foreign exchange earned by the importing country on a multinational trading basis. However, the state trading nations of Eastern Europe when part of the former Soviet Union found it convenient for planning purposes to conclude bilateral trading agreements with other countries. Under such agreements the sale of goods from (say) Uruguay to Poland would be paid for out of the proceeds of goods sold by Poland to Uruguay. The intention in the conclusion of these agreements would be that trade would be in balance over the period as a whole, but many factors can lead to unforeseen alterations to the trading pattern in the short term, and from time to time substantial bilateral credit surpluses built up.

Through negotiation it is sometimes possible for such balances to be used in settlement of trade with third countries who also conduct business with both parties to the agreement. Because the funds are switched between various countries, as are the goods, these transactions became known as switch trading and, among the categories of countertrade, none provides better justification for the earlier assertion that it must only be undertaken with the advice and assistance of experienced specialists.

Evidence accounts

In considering bilateral agreements we are thinking predominantly of state trading economies. In capitalist economies a similar situation may arise for exporters conducting a significant degree of continuing business with a country seeking to foster its own trade. As a condition of importing free from restraint there may be agreement that a percentage of exports will be matched by the exporter purchasing goods as countertrade. It is probable, with the volumes involved, that it will be impossible to match each export against a corresponding import and, in consequence, the exporter will maintain an evidence account through which will be passed the exports and imports concluded over a period, thus facilitating the achievement of an in balance situation over the term of the agreement.

Trading with Eastern Europe

Understandably, exporters have rightly regarded countertrade as being a feature of trade with Eastern Europe but have assumed that with the wane of Communism the position will automatically change. While Eastern European countries are endeavouring, with the aid of capitalist advisers, to introduce free enterprise into their economies it should be remembered that despite the change in politics they will continue to face an extreme shortage of foreign exchange for the immediate future. While this may or may not be relieved through aid, it will be some years before the position alters. For these reasons it may well be that countertrade will feature in dealings with the former Soviet Bloc for some time.

Multinational Companies and Direct Investment

If countertrade is the method by which direct export to nations short of foreign exchange resources can take place, direct investment is the alternative way through which the problem may be approached. This is not to say that direct investment is always confined to countries having liquidity problems; indeed a great deal of investment takes place in industrialized markets, particularly by multinational companies. The reasons for contemplating direct investment, which covers acquisitions, takeovers, joint ventures and the formation of subsidiary companies abroad, are varied and in one sense may be summarized as either by choice or by necessity.

A company which has been directly exporting to a market may decide that the volumes have so increased or the transport costs escalated, to the point where local manufacture is desirable particularly if the costs of such manufacture are less than those of manufacturing at home. Marketing research may show that further expansion in a market is conditional upon having a local presence or ability to produce. Both of these are examples of investment by choice.

In some instances however the decision is motivated by the imposition of prohibitive import duties, quotas or tariffs which effectively prevent direct exports and are probably designed to foster embryonic industries in the country in question. Where multinational companies are concerned an approach may be made to them indicating that an investment would be welcome to the country in question and would receive assistance in a number of ways, whereas the continuance of imports could create problems. These would be examples of investment by necessity.

The advantages which may lie in direct investment may be summarized as:

1 Access to inexpensive local supplies of raw materials may be secured.
2 Labour requirements may be satisfied readily and cheaply if a pool of skilled or semi-skilled workers exists.
3 The employment prospects arising may be of great appeal to the host country as may also the possibilities of exporting the finished products, thus earning valuable foreign exchange.
4 Incentives including favourable taxation concessions, investment grants and low interest on finance may be offered to attract investors.
5 The investment may be seen to assist the host country both by creating indigenous industry or commerce and furthering any policy of import substitution.
6 A competitive edge may be gained by being able to offer extremely short delivery times or an opportunity for any customer enquiries or complaints to be dealt with in the buyer's country.

7 The possibility of increasing markets by including those which might not be exploitable through direct exporting. (This is particularly attractive when existing markets including that in the exporter's own country, are restricted, contracting or saturated.)

8 Many host countries are eager to acquire technical expertise and will welcome investment in joint ventures (and sometimes subsidiaries) in order to achieve that aim.

9 The investor is given considerable flexibility in the allocation of resources and, on occasion taxation arrangements, by undertaking direct investment.

Possible disadvantages to direct investment are:

1 The danger to the host country that production level fluctuations and price adjustments may take place within an investing group conducting multinational operations, in order to maximize profits by concentrating on low tax benefits.

2 Relations may be soured with the host country if it is thought that insufficient percentages of profits made by the local company are being ploughed back to further its development.

3 The risk of restrictions being placed on repatriation of profits or capital should political or balance of payments problems arise.

To minimize these risks it is recommended that would-be investors should ensure, when applying for the approval of authorities in the host country for the investment to be made, that they are made aware of the investor's intentions and philosophy. Once agreed the intentions declared should be carried through and if, for some unforeseen reason, changes have to be considered, these should again be discussed with the authorities as early as possible. To cover themselves in the event of adverse regulations being applied, despite the investor having taken the precautions advised above, investors should consider insurance with the Export Credits Guarantee Department whose functions are described in chapter 2.

International Organizations Seeking to Facilitate World Trade

If the law of comparative costs were able to operate unimpeded and natural forces allowed to determine trade, as would be the case in a perfect environment, governmental intervention would not arise. However, as we are only too well aware, many considerations including national security, protection of infant industries and balance of payments difficulties, not to mention political pressures exerted by both industry and agriculture, have conspired to restrict trade.

Restrictions have taken various forms including tariffs, quotas, duties, minimum credit terms and embargoes on goods of a particular origin. To these are added the complications to world trade arising from advances in technology; for example the development of substitutes for some products and the effects on trade in the originals. Safety considerations rightly involve specifications in the buyer's country with which the exporter's products must comply but unfortunately these are seldom agreed on a worldwide basis. Health regulations are similarly necessary to protect consumers but, once more, these can vary from country to country with consequent hazards to trade. It is also unfortunately open to countries to introduce regulations on such matters as packaging, labelling and other presentational aspects which they contend are for consumer protection but other countries may see as a method by which domestic industry is protected from competition.

Thus there are many obstacles to worldwide free trade but, paradoxically, practically every country pays at least lip service to the maxim that international trade can only prosper and grow if the constraints are progressively removed through a continuing dialogue designed to find mutually agreeable solutions.

This general accord is manifested in cooperative efforts to achieve the liberalization of international trade. The consideration of these efforts is perhaps simplified by dividing the resulting international bodies into two groups, the first being aimed at removing barriers, other than financial difficulty in the importing country, to freer trade. The second group seeks to provide financial solutions by way of loans or specialist advice concerning problems of liquidity and shortage of foreign exchange. It is accepted that in the very nature of their joint aims of liberalization the work of the two groups may overlap but the distinction may help us to realize that, as in our everyday lives, purchases may be influenced either by our inability to afford a particular item or a reluctance for other reasons to purchase.

In this chapter we shall review the organizations included in the first group, the second group being included in our examination of balance of payments considerations in chapter 2. The principal organization in the first group, and one which is truly international as distinct from regional groupings seeking freer trade within their own membership, is the General Agreement on Tariffs and Trade or GATT as it is commonly termed.

The General Agreement on Tariffs and Trade (GATT)

GATT commenced its operations in 1948 following its signature in Geneva in 1947. Regular rounds or conferences are held in different parts of the world and some notable reductions in tariffs and prevention of increases to tariffs have been achieved in furtherance of its principal aims. These include most favoured nation status for its members and non discrimination in any new restrictions.

The organization has, over its history, adopted a practical approach to the issues involved, many of which are emotive. No attempt was made initially to outlaw the restrictive practices in existence prior to its inception thereby avoiding immediate antagonism. GATT preferred to induce change gradually as practices came up for review or required new arrangements due to the constantly altering trading scene arising from new technological or other developments. Flexibility is also allowed to new members in maintaining restrictions which are the result of balance of payments problems. The hope is that these will be solved eventually even though this may take a considerable time.

The same practical approach is apparent in regard to the

emergent countries in the Third World (LDCs) who as members have dispensations to apply import restrictions in support of their nascent industries. The overlap with organizations seeking to provide financial assistance in support of the furtherance of world trade is well illustrated in the cooperation between GATT, the World Bank and the International Monetary Fund, all of whom may be simultaneously assisting a country with balance of payments difficulties.

A measure of the success of GATT has been the substantial tariff reductions secured in bilateral agreements between the United Kingdom, the United States and the European Community during the Dillon Round which resulted in concessions by all countries covering trade valued at £2 bn. This was followed by concessions amounting to some $30 bn during the Kennedy Round and a rationalization of imported valuations based on transaction value in the Tokyo Round. Not surprisingly, as further concessions are negotiated, the remaining general issues are assuming a hard core nature and the task of GATT becomes more difficult. Strong expressions of feeling over agriculture, primary products and textiles in the recent Uruguay Round highlight this problem.

Apart from these Rounds which attract perhaps too much publicity, making negotiations more difficult, GATT is dealing on a day to day basis with individual restrictions which may be the result of circumstances affecting individual members.

Regional Organizations Seeking Liberalization

Paradoxically the General Agreement on Tariffs and Trade often faces problems on the worldwide question of trade restrictions due to the entrenched positions which are taken up by regional groupings formed for the purpose of liberalizing trade between their members. While tariffs are reduced or even eliminated within these groups, members adopt a common external tariff which controls imports into any member state, and lobbies within one or more members exert considerable pressure on the group to resist the lowering of these tariff walls against outsiders.

A number of free trade areas have been created in various parts of the world but, for the United Kingdom exporter, the single market programme of the European Community is of prime importance. The proportion of United Kingdom exports to the present fellow members of the Community as compared with total worldwide exports of the United Kingdom rose from 32 per cent in 1972 to over 50 per cent in 1990, and the corresponding import figure proportion from 34 per cent in 1972 to 53 per cent in 1990. Briefly then, what is the Community, its aims and structures?

The European Community

The Community originated in the Treaty of Rome, signed in 1958, which enshrined the vision of creating a single common market. The core of the market, as with other similar regional groupings, is the freeing of trade between members from tariff and quota restrictions and this has now been achieved.

The Community has also realized that trade can be restricted by impediments to the free movement of goods such as national standards, restrictions on capital or labour flows between members and subsidies or public purchasing policies pursued by individual nations. Liberalization within these fields has not yet been completed but an indication of the Community's sincerity and determination to that end is that nearly 200 measures have now been agreed which cumulatively cover nearly two thirds of the liberalization programme envisaged.

In an endeavour to produce a form of monetary union which would, it was hoped, initially promote exchange rate stability and ultimately, as an expressed aim of some but by no means all of the members, a single currency, the Community set up the European Monetary System. This comprised the European Exchange Rate Mechanism (ERM) and the European Currency Unit (ECU). More will be said about this system and the effects of the ERM on the Pound Sterling during the crisis of September 1992, which was the first major test of the system, when we examine in chapter 4 the risks exporters face from exchange rate fluctuations.

Although the concept of an enlarged domestic market is a highly attractive one it is unwise to equate selling to (say) Glasgow with sales to Milan or Athens. Agreed duties no longer complicate trade, but as regards payment, our main concern in this book, much depends on understanding the preferences, traditions and trade usages common in other member countries of the Community which are not always the same as our own. Initially the new exporter will also know less of its potential buyer in (say) Italy or France, in comparison with the experience built up over many years of trading with buyers in the United Kingdom.

Despite the ease of modern international communications the personal visit to iron out a difficulty which has arisen is not quite so simple, and this is particularly so where payment is delayed. This is not to suggest that trade should not be sought; the opportunities of the single market are immense and a challenge to be accepted, but the professional will ensure that the necessary preparatory work is carried out to maximize the chances of success.

The initial members of the Community in 1958 were Belgium, France, Germany, Holland, Italy and Luxembourg and in 1959 a second European Grouping, the European Free Trade Association (EFTA) was formed by Austria, Britain, Denmark, Norway, Portugal, Sweden and Switzerland. While EFTA's aims were broadly similar to those of the European Community, the attraction of the major markets included in the latter were a constant temptation to EFTA members. Britain in particular had considerable trade with the Community and, after abortive negotiations to join in 1961, finally joined the Community on the 1 January 1973 together with the Irish Republic and Denmark. The present membership of 12 was completed by the accession of Greece in 1980 and Portugal and Spain in 1986.

2

Country and Buyer Risk

Country Risk ✓

The first hazard facing a company which has verified that it has an exportable product, one for which there exists a healthy demand in one or more countries overseas and is not by its nature unexportable (such as a wine that will not travel or armaments for which an export licence is unobtainable), is the risk which may be inherent in exporting to the country or countries selected as having maximum commercial potential. This is known as country risk. Conventionally this risk has been considered as having two aspects, Economic and Political, being categories or circumstances which determine the level of risk applying in a particular country. I am inclined to add a third aspect – organizational – which would apply to those countries having so different a method of trading from that familiar to the nationality of the exporter as to constitute an inherent risk.

An assertion with which I believe all experienced in the export trade would agree is that the importance of researching an overseas market cannot be over-emphasized. That research can be confined to the degree of demand for the product and the most effective method of breaking into the market. These areas and the accompanying need to identify the correct distribution methods are indeed vital and the subject of other books in this series, but our concern is to stress the equally essential need to research the financial country risk. To do this we must

first understand the way in which countries express their financial position. The national equivalent of a company's annual
accounts to which we turn in order to discover if a company
is in a satisfactory position is its balance of payments. This is
normally produced on an annual basis, but alas less frequently
by a number of less developed countries.

Balance of Payments

The principle underlying a balance of payments is not dissimilar
to that which we adopt in managing a company's affairs. It seeks
to identify all income the nation derives from its financial dealings with the rest of the world; dividing this into trading receipts
and capital items. Similarly, its outgoings internationally both
in settlements for trade and capital expenditure are listed, the
resultant figure being a surplus if receipts exceed expenditure
or a deficit if expenditure exceeds receipts. This represents an
addition to or subtraction from the national reserves which corresponds to the amount that might be held in bank or building
society deposits or other assets.

The balance of payments of the United Kingdom will be
examined remembering that, while it is more sophisticated
in content than that of many less developed countries which
may constitute a country risk to United Kingdom importers, the
implications of the figures are similar. In particular an invariable
rule is that a country's creditors (which includes the cumulative
total of all its importers' creditors) wish to be paid ultimately
in their own currency or in such a form as may be freely
convertible into that currency. This is achieved at its simplest
by selling to another country an equivalent value of goods as
that imported from the country, thus achieving a balance of
payments with them. Naturally this is seldom achieved and a
surplus or deficit in trading is the normal outcome. However in
its cumulative dealings with other countries, the debtor country
must either achieve equilibrium, use its reserves or borrow foreign
currencies in order to effect settlement.

In the United Kingdom's balance of payments' figures appear
the customary three components: trade (the balance of visible

trade in goods), invisibles and capital items. Customs returns are
made of goods exported from and imported into the United
Kingdom with values calculated on a comparable basis for both
imports and exports. Although for technical reasons such figures
may contain some inaccuracies these are corrected subsequently
when fuller analysis has been completed. The trade figures are
regularly published and are used by both politicians and the
media as indicators of the nation's economic health. Because
the United Kingdom has traditionally been a net provider of
services to overseas countries the balance of invisible trade has
been particularly significant in its balance of payments and until
recent years has usually converted a deficit on the trade balance
into a surplus. While the number of items comprising invisibles
is considerable, the following are among the most important.

1 Insurance and banking. The City of London's historical
   position as the leading world financial centre has meant
   earnings under this heading have significantly surpassed
   outgoings, but the rise of competing centres has reduced the
   surplus.
2 Tourism. Many countries, including the United Kingdom,
   have increasingly appreciated the potential of the tourist
   industry in attracting foreign currency. In consequence the
   publicity given to the industry has become much greater and
   the facilities devoted to tourist development enhanced.
3 Transport of goods. The major contribution made to invisibles
   in the past through the business entrusted by foreigners to
   United Kingdom shipping lines and airlines has declined with
   the contraction of the British merchant fleet and is no longer a
   significant factor.
4 Investment. There are large flows of income derived from
   both the direct investments abroad by multinationals and
   portfolio investment in shares by UK purchasers; this is not
   comparable in significance to the amount of investment and
   the consequent income flow in the early part of this century.
5 Overseas residents. Although the contribution made to the
   invisible income of the United Kingdom by the receipt of
   remittances from its residents living or working abroad to
   dependents in this country is in no way comparable to that

in some other countries with large overseas worker ratios, it still affects the figures. A similar effect on outward invisibles arises from remittances abroad by foreign nationals employed in the United Kingdom.

The final components in the balance of payments are the capital account transactions which are distinct from the current account items comprising the trade and invisible balances already discussed. A substantial contributor to the capital account and one of considerable concern to those endeavouring to maintain stability in the management of a country's international finances, is the movement of volatile funds seeking the highest interest rate on offer at a particular time. This hot money is unpredictable in its flows and while of temporary assistance to a Chancellor endeavouring to balance his books, can prove a major destabilizing factor when withdrawn since its effect on the confidence of commercial trading holders of the currency is unpredictable. The capital account is also affected by borrowing or lending in foreign currencies by the public or private sectors in world financial markets. Borrowing will, if converted into sterling, enhance the country's reserves while the servicing of such borrowing by way of interest and repayments will have the effect of reducing reserves.

A country cannot indefinitely remain in deficit and, while drawings on reserves and borrowing overseas are temporary expedients, a more permanent solution must be sought. Natural forces may be of some help; when a deficit is created and the country's currency is subject to a system of floating exchange rates the result will be a decline in confidence in the currency leading to a progressive depreciation in its value. With fixed exchange rates a similar situation will be reached but through a deliberate devaluation by the country concerned. In either event the effect should be a stimulus to exports as foreigners find goods cheaper in their market and a simultaneous contraction of imports which will be more expensive to the debtor nation, as the country in deficit is termed. However this natural balancing process, although theoretically capable of returning the country to a position of equilibrium, is seldom deemed sufficiently sophisticated, effective or speedy to resolve the situation, particularly in less developed countries having few potential exports and the authorities will resort to other measures to achieve balance. These are a considerable concern to exporters abroad who may find them a substantial deterrent to imports into the debtor nation.

As there are many different causes for a deficit arising and in consequence differing remedies, let us look separately at industrialized countries and those of the third world, although certain of the causes and remedies will be common to both. Industrialized countries may incur deficits due to an upsurge in imports, probably reflecting preferences in taste for an overseas product or a desire to increase the variety of goods rather than through an overall lack of consumer products; this may be coupled with a weakening in their industrial base resulting in both a decrease in domestic products and a threat to exports. Equally possible is a deficit whose cause is capital-related, for example a radical change in the proportion of direct capital investment abroad as compared with the amount of inward direct investment being attracted.

In view of the restraints placed on countries which are members of the General Agreement on Tariffs and Trade, on measures designed to curb or distort international trade including the imposition of import controls or the establishment of export incentives, industrialized countries tend to try to correct deficits by controlling money supply. This correction may be accomplished through a rise in interest rates, attracting hot money and also encouraging consumers to abandon or at least postpone expenditure, perhaps accompanied by a rise in taxation. It may also take the form of adopting credit controls which can be directed at borrowers, such as minimum down payments on goods purchased on credit, or at banks and other providers of credit by restricting the amount of funds available to lend. These methods have the effect of reducing demand. It must however be said that the often conflicting aims of achieving international financial stability and domestic prosperity provide a severe test for those controlling monetary policy.

In less developed countries the problem, although similar in that imports increase to an extent which is not fundable by exports, has subtle differences. The outflow of foreign exchange occasioned by the increased imports is frequently enhanced by the cost of servicing international indebtedness and the demand for imports arises from a lack of basic consumer goods as distinct from a desire to increase variety of choice within an already substantial supply. The corrective measures in these countries therefore focus primarily on controlling the entry of imports and conserving reserves of foreign exchange. Import controls include duties, licensing and the imposition of quotas, frequently concentrating on selectivity by allowing a continuing inflow of basic needs but progressively restricting less essential goods, culminating in the total prohibition of luxury goods.

The International Monetary Fund and the World Bank

In chapter 1 we observed that, in the context of furthering the growth of world trade, two groups of international bodies have been established; the first is concerned with removing obstacles to freer trade and the second with providing finance and advice to countries with liquidity problems and foreign exchange shortages. This latter group of organizations plays a vital part in endeavouring to solve balance of payments crises and is of importance to the exporter researching country risk in so far as their involvement or non-involvement may determine the severity and duration of the crises, and they may offer finance to the country concerned in supporting basic projects requiring foreign participation.

During the period from the abandoning of the gold standard to the beginning of World War II movements in exchange rates compared with those occurring in the last fifty years were modest. Some efforts were made from time to time to control what were considered as excess fluctuations but these official interventions in foreign exchange markets were neither supported by other monetary devices nor coordinated internationally. It was only during the closing years of the war that recognition of problems likely to occur began to take place;

these led to the Bretton Woods international monetary conference which considered the effects of exchange rate movements on trade. The result was a conclusion that fluctuations were indeed detrimental to the growth of world trade and the establishment of two bodies, membership of which could be sought by any interested nation. The first was the International Monetary Fund (IMF) and the second was the International Bank for Reconstruction and Development (commonly known as the World Bank).

The early years of operation were difficult as the distortions in wealth between nations resulting from the war far out-weighed any which could have been foreseen by those attending Bretton Woods. However the most significant decision was to introduce fixed exchange rates with a tolerance of 1 per cent (later broadened to 2.25 per cent) on either side of a parity rate (not dissimilar it may be said to the concept underlying the Exchange Rate Mechanism of the European Community discussed in a later chapter). The strains on the system, which compelled devaluation or revaluation upwards, as a decision by the authorities, if the fixed rate became unsupportable due to changes in world confidence, became too great and in 1972 floating rates of exchange which allowed gradual reaction to pressures caused by confidence factors were restored.

While readers wishing to obtain a detailed knowledge of the aims and methods of operation of the International Monetary Fund and the World Bank are advised to refer to the Articles of Agreement, exporters' interest in learning how the organizations seek to limit balance of payment difficulties and thus the extent of country risk should be satisfied by a summary of the provisions.

The International Monetary Fund aimed through international collaboration and consultation to recognize and seek solutions to monetary problems and thus facilitate the development of the productive resources of its members. Exchange stability, orderly exchange arrangements and the avoidance of competitive exchange depreciation were sought with the object of eliminating foreign exchange restrictions which were rightly seen as hampering the growth of world trade. This it was hoped would 'shorten the duration and lessen the degree of disequilibrium in the international balance of payments of members'. A further objective, of particular relevance to exporters seeking to maintain exports to countries experiencing balance of payments difficulties, was that the fund would make its general resources available to such countries on a temporary basis in order that an opportunity was thereby given to correct maladjustments without the need to resort to measures 'destructive to national or international prosperity'.

The fund operates with subscriptions paid by members in acceptable currencies, including that of the member, and SDRs (special drawing rights); the amount of the subscription being fixed in relation to the member country's economic importance internationally, and subject to periodic review. These subscriptions can be augmented in case of emergencies by loans to the fund by selected countries who agreed in principle to such support being offered. The fund's resources are made available to applicant members through a system of quotas reviewed at five yearly intervals. The quota allocated to each member equals the amount of its subscription. If a member encounters balance of payment problems and has exhausted its normal supplies of foreign currency to deal with these it may apply for currency from the fund up to the maximum permissible, which is 200 per cent of the quota, or such greater amount as the Fund, at its discretion, may authorize.

The member will use its own currency or other acceptable means (such as gold) to purchase the amount taken in excess of quota and strict conditions are imposed designed to accomplish repurchase by the member of its own currency from the fund in the shortest possible time. It is also usual for countries applying for assistance to involve the International Monetary Fund in consideration of the causes for the crisis and suggestions for how it can be resolved, often resulting in a plan being drawn up jointly with the Fund specifying action to be taken. This not only renders expert advice available to the applicant but also is increasingly regarded by those with whom it trades as representing evidence of its sincerity of intent in pursuing remedial action. The International Monetary Fund has a current membership exceeding 140 countries which between them are responsible for most world trade.

The World Bank in its early years grappled with the financial problems arising internationally from the aftermath of the Second World War which left both victors and vanquished with the need to rebuild their economies and trade. Currently its main role in assisting investment by the provision of loans and guarantees is heavily weighted towards less developed countries and concentrates on those projects which are considered to facilitate long term improvements in infrastructure and thereby improve the very low living standards which normally exist. One of the World Bank's main virtues is that loans are frequently made in circumstances where private investors would be hesitant to accept the inherent risks. It is strongly desirable for exporters to obtain information at as early a stage as possible regarding loans which are contemplated as this may offer the only chance of business with the recipient country; the loans generally being 'untied' to any particular supplier.

In similar fashion to the advice offered to members by the International Monetary Fund on balance of payments problems as part of financial assistance, the World Bank will use the considerable pool of specialists in various areas of industry, agriculture, and public works available to it as advisors to the would be borrower (and lender) to ensure that development is effectively planned over a period and the finance used to maximum benefit. Loans made by the bank are on commercial terms as regards interest charged but with repayment maturity dates of up to 25 years and involve sovereign risk, being guaranteed by the government of the borrowing country.

Funding for World Bank operations consists of subscriptions from its membership of over 140 nations, based as in the case of the International Monetary Fund on their economic standing, but more importantly through the issue of its bonds in principal financial centres throughout the world.

The summary of international institutions offering financial help in the interests of world trade and investment would not be complete without reference to the International Finance Corporation (IFC) and the International Development Association (IDA), which are both affiliates of the World Bank, and the Commonwealth Development Finance Company. The intention in setting up the two affiliates was to broaden the range of loans and type of projects eligible for assistance, this being achieved through lending specialities in each institution. As we have seen, the World Bank specializes in loans up to 25 years on commercial terms which are made against sovereign risk. The International Finance Corporation complements these initiatives by financing acceptable private sector projects in less developed countries without government guarantee, while the International Development Association completes the range by offering assistance up to 50 years interest free for selected projects which offer outstanding benefits to less developed countries. Both affiliates rely on the World Bank to fund assistance offered.

The Commonwealth Development Finance Company also works closely with the World Bank but has different parentage being sponsored by a variety of financial institutions following the Commonwealth Economic Conference in 1952. The assistance given is to Commonwealth countries and the range of projects supported are broadly similar to those favoured by the International Finance Corporation.

Political Risk

Thus far we have looked at the economic aspect of country risk; the danger to an exporter entering a market which is, for a variety of reasons, actually or potentially financially unsound in its international balance of payments. A quite distinct component in country risk is the political aspect. This can arise from either internal or external factors. The most obvious is an unstable government or one which is known to have policies which are opposed to imports and (or) direct investment from abroad. The former is particularly of concern if the anticipated alternative government has restrictive policies. In such circumstances the exporter or investor may experience sudden impositions of exchange controls or import restrictions and it is by no means unknown for these to be applied retrospectively in extreme cases. An internal security problem can contribute to political risk by threatening conveyance of the goods, increasing the costs of transport and insurance and, if the insurrection is sufficiently widespread, creating economic risk by diverting resources which could have sustained trade into maintaining law and order.

External factors affecting political risk are diverse but include such well-known cases as the Israeli/Arab longstanding dispute and the basically ethnic disputes which have characterized the breaking up of the previous nations of Yugoslavia and the Soviet Union. The latter also illustrates that political risk may not be confined to systems which are alien to that applying in the exporter's country.

When the communists ruled in Eastern Europe although trade was fettered by a slow and cumbersome method of state control and country risk might well have been within the third category mentioned earlier, where organizational procedures can drive an exporter into financial danger, payments were almost invariably made promptly when due – an observation which could not be made in regard to many capitalist economies. Now the system is being converted to one more closely identified with capitalism the initial changes will have a traumatic effect on individual enterprises which will be exposed to situations from which they were previously shielded by the same organizations acting as both negotiators and distributors. The teething problems which will undoubtably result can be properly described as a constituent of the political country risk to which the exporter is exposed.

Buyer Risk

Buyer risk is a concept far more familiar to the average company, whether it is exporting or not, than is country risk. Although loosely speaking companies do have a country risk in dealing in the domestic market, for example that of the government changing monetary policy in such a way as to kill demand for a particular product, it is rarely consciously identified. Buyer risk however is well appreciated by every company; it is the specific risk associated with selling to individual buyers as distinct from that of selling to the market as a whole. The two elements comprising buyer risk are the ability and willingness of the purchaser to settle; the 'can't pay' and 'won't pay' response. It is extremely important to separate the two as the sources from which the exporter will seek information during his preparatory work are quite different.

In banking it is an old and trusted maxim that when lending to a customer his character is the paramount factor, the security he provides secondary. If he is dishonest, no matter how satisfactory the collateral the loan is likely to be a constant source of trouble. The same principle applies concerning exports – if the buyer does not act in good faith there will be similar problems; the quality of goods supplied may be questioned, the transport arrangements and delivery terms disputed, the contract of sale scrutinized for possible loopholes, and payment delayed or refused for no valid reason.

Thus it is essential that the exporter seeks opinions from informed sources on the trading morality of the buyer. If the order has been routed through an agent whose responsibilities include vetting the potential buyer the necessary enquiries should have been made. If the request for a quote comes direct from a would be buyer the agent may well be able to give a trade reference which is the term used to describe an opinion on trading morality. Other sources are the Department of Trade and Industry (DTI) who maintain extensive files on overseas importers built up from past experience and United Kingdom diplomatic posts abroad, chambers of commerce and trade associations, the latter being particularly useful if the product is one which demands considerable trading experience if business is to be satisfactorily concluded.

Of course the exporter may, and often does, ask the buyer for trade references. In some cases they are provided by the buyer automatically when he forwards the enquiry. These volunteered references may well be highly satisfactory in the opinion expressed and sufficient for the exporter's purpose but prudence requires the reservation to be made that a dishonest buyer would ensure that any referee volunteered would speak favourably. It is therefore preferable to make independent enquiries wherever possible. Trade references should not be regarded as indicating the subject company's financial standing and indeed they will often specifically exclude any such indication. The referee is commenting from his previous experience in trade dealings with the potential buyer on the latter's willingness to deal honestly (that he will not adopt the 'won't pay' stance), not on the financial ability or credit-worthiness of the subject.

The 'can't pay' risk is researched by the exporter through enquiries addressed to either banks or credit agencies and these should be regarded as complementary to trade references and not as a substitute. The choice between bank and credit agency as a source for financial information is for the exporter to make; in either case well established institutions should prove satisfactory and, if the exporter desires, approaches can be made to both banks and agencies. An agency will collate factual information from a wide selection of sources and there is keen competition in inviting requests for reports, through stressing a particular agency's ability to access the highest possible number of data bases internationally. The information tends to be greater in amount and detail than that normally provided by a bank and frequently includes significant data voluntarily contributed by the subject together with relevant excerpts from the annual accounts where available.

Bank's reports are normally opinions which are given based on their experience of the subject's account up to the date the enquiry is received. It is important that the reader differentiates between bank reports (or status enquiries) sought by UK sellers on buyers resident in the UK and those sought by exporters on overseas buyers as a significant change in UK banking practice has taken effect as from the 28th March 1994. Thereafter, UK sellers seeking bank reports on UK buyers must apply **direct to the buyer's bank** including in their request **written consent from the buyer** for their bankers to provide the information. Such requests must also state the nature of the transaction on which the opinion is required and include payment of the tariff charge of the bank for the service.

The system for UK exporters seeking bank reports on their overseas buyers is that the request should be made **to the exporter's bank in the UK** quoting (if known) the name of the buyer's bank. The UK bank will communicate the request to the bank abroad whose reply will be sent by the UK bank on receipt to the exporter. **No consent of the buyer** to the report being given is required to accompany the request and the exporter's account will normally be debited with the charges of both banks for the service provided.

It is common for the wording of reports to be in guarded terms, traditionally used, which are not always as immediately clear to the exporter as might be wished. In seeking bank reports it is important that one asks the question to which one requires the reply. The request for a report (status enquiry) on an overseas buyer may seek either a general or specific question to be asked. The general is well suited to the stage when an exporter first attempts to explore a market or to expand into new markets; the commercial demand has been verified and a provisional list of possible agents, distributors or direct buyers established. The company's sales representatives are poised to visit the market(s) and wish to use their time to best advantage in selecting from the list those companies who should receive priority calls. A reply to a request for a general report on a company might include: 'Respectably constituted company. We do not consider they would enter into any commitment they were unable to fulfil.'

For the purpose envisaged this would be perfectly acceptable as it indicates the bank has a favourable opinion of its customer. It would however be inadequate and possibly irritating to the exporter seeking to determine if an enquiry from the same customer for a stated value of goods, on a suggested credit term should be given a favourable response. In that event a specific request for a status enquiry (bank report) should be made by the exporter to his bank. An example might be a request for a report on the XYZ company as to whether they are considered good for payment for machinery value £75,000 in a single shipment payable by bills of exchange drawn at 90 days sight. In most cases a favourable response to such an enquiry will include: 'Considered good for your figure and purpose.'

There are no international rules governing the wording to be used in replying to status enquiries, and the amount of information supplied may vary considerably from country to country. However in giving their opinions, as distinct from providing any supplementary particulars on the subject, banks have a number of well used phrases which are worthy of a few words of explanation for those not familiar with the jargon or emphasis to be attributed.

'Considered undoubted (for its obligations)' is a report which cannot be bettered. Remember banks are traditionally cautious and will only use words such as 'undoubted' if their opinion is that any exporter should have absolute confidence in the subject's financial integrity.

'Respectably constituted company. We do not consider they would enter into any commitment they were unable to fulfil but the figures quoted are higher than those normally seen' is both complimentary and cautionary. The bank clearly considers its customer a company whose financial trading morality is established and this reply would certainly not be given if the bank's experience was of regular delays or defaults in settlement. However it is endeavouring to indicate that its experience is of somewhat smaller purchases as the norm. The circumstances in which this abnormally large order is contemplated are probably unknown to the bank; it might be that the importer is keen to increase stocks in view of an impending price rise or has an end buyer who has already given a firm order for the entire shipment. The bank recognizes these reasonable trading possibilities and its reply shows it does not consider any such exceptional order would lead to a dishonoured commitment, but it is implying that if normal orders were to be raised to the sort of figure mentioned in the status enquiry the bank would not necessarily be prepared to give an unqualified favourable response. Often this type of reply will cause the exporter to pause for thought and perhaps suggest the phasing of the delivery of the order in such a way that only a portion of the total amount remains outstanding at any one time, the earlier deliveries having been paid for.

We have seen that bankers' reports are based on their experience of the subject's account and not on hearsay or even on information obtained from reputable sources which have a long association with the company. It follows therefore that if the bank has held the account for only a limited time it will feel bound to qualify any opinion accordingly. Such a scenario could be indicated by a report such as: 'Our experience with the subject, although entirely satisfactory, is limited'. There could, however, be an alternative and perhaps more ominous interpretation of this comment.

The bank may have observed that, although the account has been in existence for some time, very little business has been seen. Has the subject another account with a second bank, covering the majority of its trading, which is perhaps not so satisfactory and would not bring forth a strong status report were requests to be received? It was noted when commenting on trade references that a referee suggested by a buyer might not always be representative, and a similar observation is valid if the banking referee is nominated. It could be only one of a number of banks holding accounts for the subject but the one through which solely transactions of an 'entirely satisfactory' nature are directed. The advice for an exporter receiving the type of reply quoted or any other wording implying a short or limited banking relationship with the subject is to obtain further financial assessments, perhaps through a credit agency and to pay even greater attention to the trade references as a guide to general trading morality.

'Dealings are recommended on a secured basis' reflects the cautious banker who is concerned (possibly very concerned) at the financial state of his customer. Even if the banker feels the subject is in such dire straits as to be basically insolvent and that the appointment of a receiver is imminent, considerations of confidentiality preclude saying so. Instead is used this form of report which to the experienced reader tells all and ensures that the recipient, experienced or not, can be in no doubt that if he enters into any transaction on an unsecured basis the risk is entirely his and no recourse could possibly be made to the bank on the basis of its report implying that all was well. However, as we shall discover when considering methods of payment in a later chapter, there are various degrees of security present in various forms of settlement and the status report quoted would normally imply a letter of credit being sought from the buyer.

One or two misconceptions, which occur frequently concerning bankers reports, merit comment. Is a banker influenced in his report by the value or longstanding relationship with the subject? The answer is no, any banker basing his report on other than his experience of the account, whether the customer's business is profitable or not and the relationship dates over five or one hundred years, does so at his peril. Is the enquirer entitled to revert to the bank in the event of the buyer failing to pay? This is a much more difficult question to answer and for an informed opinion on the legal position the exporter should take appropriate advice.

However, common sense requires some investigation in advance of such an approach. Clearly the conditions of the sales contract must have been fulfilled in every respect by the exporter, leaving no possibility of the buyer offering non-performance as a reason for withholding payment. The justification for any reversion to the bank must also depend on whether this is a 'won't pay' or 'can't pay' situation. The former assumes the probability of the buyer raising some obstacle, imagined or otherwise, to settlement on this particular occasion. The bank can hardly be expected to have foreseen such an eventuality, far less to have allowed for it in the opinion given. The buyer who is unable to pay presents a quite different situation. Is his inability due to factors beyond his personal financial position? Here the most obvious example is the buyer residing in a country whose authorities impose exchange control regulations or a moratorium on debt settlements due to foreign exchange shortages. As we have observed in this chapter, this is a case of country and not buyer risk and thus any question of querying the bank's opinion does not arise. We are left therefore with the case of a buyer who becomes insolvent prior to making payment to the exporter.

Leaving aside the legal position, most reputable banks would accept that they are morally responsible for opinions given in response to status enquiries. The opinion is however similar to a photograph, in that it portrays the subject's position **at a given point in time** as it appears to the bank from the information then before it. It follows that the success of any claim for loss resulting from the exporter having relied on the bank's report must depend on events between the time the report is given and that at which the default occurs. If there has been a steady decline in the buyer's financial position which started prior to the report and continued thereafter it might be contended that the bank should have been aware of the dangers and reported accordingly, although the longer the time between the report and the default the greater is the chance of a defence based on changing circumstances being successful. If it is apparent that an entirely unforeseeable event has occurred during that time – such as the cancellation of a major order – which has caused the insolvency then the bank is unlikely to accept any responsibility.

The last misconception in regard to status enquiries again concerns time. Bankers are all too familiar with financial crises which have overtaken their customers due to a buyer's default on payment for a major order. During the ensuing discussion the question is asked: 'Was a status report sought on the buyer?'. The answers, if somewhat disappointing, are informative. The majority have probably requested financial reports either from a bank or a credit agency and trade references are usually obtained. Many however are content with general enquiries even if the size of the order would have appeared to have made a specific enquiry on amount and credit terms desirable.

More serious is the fact that on further enquiry it emerges that the customer has continued to rely on a report for periods measured in years rather than months. Why this assumption exists that reports remain valid over the long term is difficult to understand. We have only to look at the financial pages in our daily newspapers or indeed the opening or closing of shops in our local high street to realize the fluctuating fortunes of businesses and this is no less true on the international scene.

It is impossible to lay down hard and fast rules as to the frequency with which reports should be renewed as individual circumstances vary, but as a guide I would suggest twelve monthly as a minimum on continuing average volume business and six months for those sales which are for abnormally large amounts. In considering the interval bear in mind also that during times of recession the fluctuations in fortune are both more pronounced and more frequent than in times of prosperity and an increase in frequency of renewal may be prudent.

Credit Insurance

Despite exercising every care by thoroughly researching country and buyer risk before entering into a transaction, the exporter may face default by the buyer. In addition the exporter may not always be able to obtain the buyer's agreement to the method of payment which is preferred after a study of trade references and the replies to status enquiries; we shall recognize many times in this book that the world of international trade is extremely competitive and if the alternative is to lose the order an exporter may decide to accept a less secure method of payment. The realities of competition are frequently such that a buyer may select from a number of potential sellers and the choice may depend not only on price but on a number of other factors including credit terms, currency of quotation and the method of payment stipulated. This last factor is particularly vital in the European Single Market where buyers are extremely reluctant to deal on other than open account terms.

The exporter facing these problems may be in a position to obtain insurance against both the country and buyer risks. This type of insurance, which is known as credit insurance, should not be confused with normal commercial insurance covering risks to which the goods are exposed in transit. The insurers are usually different and the policies separate. Not only does the holding of credit insurance give peace of mind to the insured, it can also enable the exporter to compete more successfully. For example in the situation envisaged earlier of a buyer insisting on open account the exporter is more willing to concede those terms if credit insurance is held. A third benefit to be considered later under finance for exports is that a policy may assist an exporter in obtaining finance for sales abroad.

Short term cover

Not surprisingly, the vast majority of credit insurance policies (or guarantees as they are often called) are in respect of sales on credit terms up to 180 days and this short term category of business will be looked at first. Until fairly recently the bulk of short term cover in the United Kingdom was provided by a government department – the Export Credits Guarantee Department (ECGD) – which will be examined later in relation to capital goods exports and those on medium or long term credit. The short term business of ECGD has now been taken over by a Dutch group NCM (Nederlandsche Creditetverzekering Maatschappij) which now shares the market with a number of other private sector credit insurers. Although we are interested only in the services they supply to exporters, these insurers also offer similar insurance against buyer risk to firms trading in the domestic or home market.

In seeking short term cover it is important to understand the principles underlying comprehensive policies which will apply to most insurers although it is of course necessary to examine in detail the particular policy offered. The buyer and country risks are covered in a single policy which is equally appropriate to companies exporting to multiple markets or a selection of specialized markets and for the covering of low or high value shipments. While premiums will vary according to the exporter's requirements, it is important to appreciate that the lowest will be applied where a wide range of markets are offered giving a reasonable spread of risk. It is obviously unrealistic to expect an insurer to cover only exports to countries with a high risk, and even if he were to do so it would be at a very high and perhaps prohibitive premium.

Broad particulars of the risks covered are as follows but again verification should be obtained, as conditions may vary from time to time and, as regards detail, between insurers.

Country risks

1 Action by the authorities in the country the effect of which is wholly or partly to frustrate performance of the contract.
2 Economic or political events occurring outside the United Kingdom resulting in delays or prevention of payment.
3 War or insurrection outside the United Kingdom (other than war between the five major powers) frustrating performance of the contract unless such risk is coverable under commercial insurance.

4 Delays in transferring money from the buyer's country which do not result from actions of the seller or buyer.

5 The introduction of restrictions on the export of the goods involved after the signature of the sales contract, or the cancellation of an export licence valid at that time or refusal to renew such a licence.

6 In respect of buyers in the public sector or where payment is guaranteed by a public sector guarantor, the failure to perform the terms of the contract.

Buyer risk

1 Insolvency of the buyer.
2 Where goods have been accepted by the buyer, his failure to make payment within six months from the date upon which it is agreed to be due.
3 Provided goods shipped are in compliance with the contract, the buyer's failure to take delivery.

It is customary for cover to be extended to up to 90 per cent of loss in the case of buyer insolvency or default but, should the buyer fail to take delivery of the goods, the exporter is subject to an excess of 20 per cent with the insurer covering 90 per cent of the balance. For loss arising from country risk cover is up to 95 per cent. Thus in all cases the exporter is left with an interest over and above the cover provided and he is also expected to take action designed to recover the debt in conjunction with the insurer.

Having established the policy individual buyers are declared to the insurer and a credit limit given which obviates the necessity for the exporter to refer each transaction provided outstanding credit with the buyer concerned is within the limit. In relation to cash flow it is important for the exporter to be aware of any delay from the time of the loss being sustained to the payment of claims by the insurer. The following time scale for payment by NCM, provided a fully documented claim is submitted promptly and is accepted, is indicative of normal delays.

1 Immediately on proof of your buyer's insolvency.
2 Six months after due date of payment for protracted default on goods accepted.
3 One month after resale if the original buyer has failed to take up the order.
4 Four months after due date for most other causes of loss.

Credit insurance is flexible and short term cover is available for goods manufactured outside the United Kingdom as well as domestically. Invoicing in currency is permissible for cover in which case it may well be possible to insure against additional loss arising through the exporter having to honour a forward exchange contract (see chapter 4). Further flexibility is apparent in the provision of cover, upon request, for:

(a) sales through overseas subsidiaries;
(b) royalties on licensing and franchising agreements; and
(c) goods sold from stock held overseas or after exhibition.

Last but by no means of least importance to the exporter supplying specialized goods, for a particular buyer, which would have little demand in the general market, cover may be arranged from the date of contract instead of, as normal, from the date of dispatch to the buyer. This protects the exporter, in the event of the buyer's repudiation of the contract, being left with goods manufactured to specialized order which might be totally unsaleable.

Other forms of credit insurance cover

Credit insurance is not confined to exports on terms up to 180 days. Other forms of cover are available, the principal insurer being the Export Credits Guarantee Department who offer three basic services to the exporter:

1 Guarantees of payment to banks providing export finance, often where medium term credit has been extended to buyers.

2 Support for export finance at favourable fixed interest rates.

3 Insurance for non-payment on export contracts.

The first and second of these services will be described in chapter 10 as it is felt they form a part of the range of financing possibilities available to the exporter. They are therefore mentioned here solely to render complete the summary of facilities available from credit insurers. The third basic service covers a number of insurance policies (guarantees). **A Supplier Insurance Policy** is an optional extra to exporters seeking financial guarantees to their banks, and covers against both buyer and country risks arising between the signature of the contract and the time finance is provided (that is the pre-finance period). It is also possible for this policy to cover any portion of the payment price which is excluded from the financing such as an advance payment. **Specific Guarantees** cover against loss due to specified commercial and political risks preventing an exporter from receiving payments on a capital goods contract but can also cover services and constructional works contracts. Cover is normally for 90 per cent of loss suffered.

Another form of specific guarantee is an optional extra to guarantees enabling finance to be given to a buyer to provide the means for cash settlements to the exporter. This form covers the pre-finance period and losses relating to any payments due outside the financing arrangements. The **Overseas Investment Insurance Facility** provides protection to United Kingdom companies making direct investments overseas, by way of long term equity or loan, against expropriation, war and restrictions on remittances.

The final component in the third basic service is the **Tender to Contract Cover/Forward Exchange Supplement** which, because an understanding of its nature presupposes a knowledge of foreign exchange risks, is dealt with in chapter 4.

3

The Quotation

The quotation from the exporter to the potential buyer is almost certainly the most important milestone in the quest for a successful sale. It is the point where the research devoted to the various disciplines comprising the art of exporting is weighed and balanced and a decision taken as to whether the business should be pursued. This will have included an assessment of demand for the product and the requirements of the market; investigation of what responsibilities the exporter is prepared to shoulder in regard to the delivery of the goods; and the calculation of costs and profit margins.

All are translated into the quotation which is also a vital indication of the price considerations which will probably appear in any subsequent contract. It is therefore essential that from the payment viewpoint the exporter should clearly understand how the quotation is made up. If he does not then the first seeds of misconception as to the responsibilities of the parties to the contract will have been planted and, at best, disrupting arguments or, at worst, legal disputes will lie ahead.

What are the cost components making up an export price? To avoid considering in abstract let us assume an example which will also illustrate the various other aspects requiring attention. PDB Exports (93) Ltd have received an enquiry from Relay Reactions Inc., Toronto for the supply of 15,000 widgets. The initial enquiry contained copious particulars of the widgets but a response from the exporters for clarification, prior to deciding whether they were within their range of products, has produced a numbered specification dated 15th January 1993. Thus to avoid any misunderstandings regarding the goods the quotation will cover '15,000 widgets as per your specification No 1411/3 dated 15th January 1993'. The enquiry makes no reference to any suggested credit terms, although the exporter anticipates credit will be required, and neither delivery terms nor currency of quotation are mentioned.

The export transaction does not differ from the home market sale in regard to the fundamental costs which must be reflected in the price quoted. These costs comprise:

1 The cost of raw materials or components used in order to produce the end product.
2 The costs involved in manufacturing the product which can be broken down into those of labour and any which are specific to the order for which the quote is given. Examples would be special dies which might or might not have a use after completion of the order and the pro-rata costs of specialized tools or machinery not in general use.
3 Overheads – the term applied to the general costs of running a business including research and development, transport, rents and depreciation, clerical/office expenses and heat, light and power, to name but a few. These are naturally not specific to the enquiry under quote but a percentage is applied calculated on the nature of the order which may result, particularly size (affecting the amount of capacity utilized) and the estimated production time.

To these fundamental costs will be added the required profit margin which will vary from one case to another based on competitive factors, but will appear in the exporter's calculations as a percentage of the other costs. At this stage a price will have been determined which reflects basic materials and manufacturing costs plus profit, but which excludes the anticipated costs of transport, duties, agency commissions and finance should these be borne by the exporter within the terms of the agreement with the buyer, subsequently to be incorporated into the contract.

Delivery Terms

Before continuing with the build up of a quotation price it is necessary to consider what is meant by a delivery term. Depending on the degree of competition existing in the market concerned, the potential value of the order on offer and likely repeats and the wishes, if known, of the would-be buyer, the exporter will decide on the extent of responsibilities he will accept and those which he expects the buyer to undertake in respect of delivery of the goods.

It is not a question of direct financial liability as the exporter will calculate his quotation to include the expense he is incurring in accepting responsibility, but of convenience, since the formalities in arranging delivery can be onerous particularly to the small firm which will almost certainly find it necessary (and desirable) to employ the services of a freight forwarder. The division of responsibilities will be evidenced by the use of a delivery term – the agreement of which between buyer and seller will be a pre-requisite to the contract. In view of the obvious importance of delivery terms it would be most unfortunate if their wording were such as to be capable of different interpretations by the parties.

A considerable service has been rendered to the international trading community by the International Chamber of Commerce (ICC) which produced and have subsequently revised a list of delivery terms known as Incoterms which cover the vast majority of divisions of responsibility adopted by exporters and importers. It is not obligatory for any contract to refer to an Incoterm but the wise exporter will almost invariably ensure that it does for the protection of both the buyer and itself. Any student of export practice should obtain a copy of *Incoterms 1990* available from ICC Publishing S.A. (Cours Albert 1er 75008 Paris, France) or through any of the ICC National Committees (the address for the United Kingdom is 14/15 Belgrave Square, London SW1X 8PS and for the United States is 156 Fifth Avenue, New York, NY 10010, USA).

Incoterms 1990 comprises 13 terms which are arranged in four groups in an ascending order of responsibilities assumed by the seller. Each group has a key letter which appears as the first in each term appearing in that group. 'E' term is the only one in the E group and covers situations where goods are made available to the buyer at the seller's premises. The F Group includes three 'F' terms all of which apply to situations where the seller delivers goods to a carrier stipulated by the buyer. 'C' terms of which there are four, involve the seller in contracted carriage to a stipulated point but not thereafter, while the five 'D' terms in Group D place responsibility on the seller for arrival at the agreed destination. In detail the complete list of terms is:

Group E EXW Ex Works

Group F FCA Free Carrier
FAS Free Alongside Ship Main Carriage Unpaid
FOB Free on Board

Group C CFR Cost and Freight
CIF Cost, Insurance and Freight Main Carriage Paid
CPT Carriage Paid To
CIP Carriage and Insurance Paid To

Group D DAF Delivered at Frontier
DES Delivered Ex Ship
DEQ Delivered Ex Quay
DDU Delivered Duty Unpaid
DDP Delivered Duty Paid

The textbook on Incoterms 1990 contains a concise definition of each delivery term including the obligations of both parties as regards the obtaining and delivery of documentation, the transfer of risk and division of costs. In this volume our concern is with costs, but any failure to appreciate the significance of the documentation and risk transfer provisions, which are dealt with in companion books in this series, may result in misunderstandings with the buyer; to resolve these can have financial implications. Let us consider each delivery term with a view to determining the costs for which the exporter is responsible and which will therefore be incorporated in its quotation, and those which are the buyer's obligations.

Ex Works

The seller fulfils his delivery obligations upon making available at his premises to the buyer the goods normally, but not necessarily in such packing as may be reasonably required for transport to their destination, unless it is trade custom to make those particular goods available unpacked. The seller must pay the costs of packaging and of any additional operations such as weighing, counting, measuring or quality checks, necessary in order that the goods are at the disposal of the buyer. All other charges from the time of delivery at the seller's premises are the responsibility of the buyer.

FCA Free Carrier

The seller's delivery obligations are fulfilled when he has delivered goods, cleared for export, into the charge of the carrier nominated by the buyer. The seller's responsibilities for costs similarly cover all expenses necessary until such time as delivery is made to the carrier, which would include transport from the seller's premises and the costs of formalities and any duties payable on exportation. The buyer is responsible for all costs in respect of the goods from the time they are delivered to the carrier.

FAS Free Along Ship

This term determines fulfilment of the seller's obligations to deliver when the goods have been placed on the quay alongside the carrying vessel or in lighters at the port of shipment. The seller is responsible for all costs until the time such delivery is made, thereafter the buyer assumes responsibility for costs.

FOB Free on Board

The seller's delivery obligations are fulfilled immediately the goods pass over the rail of the carrying vessel at the port of shipment and responsibility for costs is confined to those incurred before that. Thereafter the buyer assumes responsibility for costs.

CFR Cost and Freight

This delivery term differentiates between the costs and freight necessary to cover shipment of the goods to the port of destination and the risk of loss of or damage to the goods after they have passed over the ship's rail at the port of shipment. The former costs, including any shipping line charges for loading or unloading, are the responsibility of the seller but the latter, as well as any additional costs due to events occurring after the goods have been delivered on board the vessel, including insurance, are the responsibility of the buyer.

CIF Cost, Insurance and Freight

This term differs from CFR only in so far as the cost of marine insurance on minimum coverage is the responsibility of the seller and not the buyer.

CPT Carriage Paid To (named place of destination)

The seller's obligation to deliver is fulfilled when the goods are in the custody of the carrier or, if there are subsequent carriers, to the first carrier for transportation to the named destination. Freight costs to that destination are the responsibility of the seller, additional costs due to events occurring after delivery of goods to the carrier that of the buyer, including insurance.

CIP Carriage and Insurance Paid To (named place of destination)

This term differs from CPT only in so far as the responsibility and costs of providing cargo insurance, covering the buyer's risk of loss or damage to the goods while being carried to the named place of destination, are those of the seller. The obligation under CIP is only to obtain insurance on minimum coverage.

DAF Delivered at Frontier (named place of destination)

This, the first of the D group terms, obliges the seller to deliver goods, cleared for export at the named place at the frontier but prior to their arriving at the customs border of the adjoining country. It is essential that the frontier concerned be defined precisely in the term as DAF may on occasion be used for goods required to be delivered at the frontier of the country of export. Costs up to the point and place of delivery, including the expenses of discharge if necessary in order to effect delivery, are the responsibility of the seller. Thereafter costs are the obligation of the buyer including customs duties and other formalities necessary to arrange importation.

DES Delivered Ex Ship

The seller's delivery obligations are fulfilled when the goods have been made available to the buyer on board the ship, uncleared for import, at the named destination. All costs until such time as such delivery is made are the responsibility of the seller.

DEQ Delivery Ex Quay (Duty Paid)

In order to fulfil its obligations the seller must make goods available to the buyer on the quay (wharf), cleared for importation, at the port of destination. The costs up to delivery including duties and taxes on import are the seller's responsibility. Considerable flexibility is possible within the delivery term. If the buyer is required to pay duty the words 'Duty Unpaid' are used instead of 'Duty Paid' and if certain of the importation costs are to be excluded from the seller's responsibilities this can be achieved by a specific mention; for example 'Delivered Ex Quay VAT Unpaid'.

DDU Delivered Duty Unpaid (named place of destination)

When goods have been made available at the named place in the country of importation the seller's delivery obligations have been fulfilled. The costs involved in bringing the goods to the named place must be borne by the seller including those of carrying out customs formalities necessary for their importation but excluding duties, taxes and official charges. Flexibility is again achievable under this delivery term in that it can be amended, should the parties agree that some of the costs payable upon importation should be borne by the seller, by the addition of suitable wording. For example 'Delivered Duty Unpaid, VAT Paid'.

DDP Delivered Duty Paid (named place of destination)

The seller's delivery obligations are identical to 'Delivered Duty Unpaid' but, in addition to its responsibilities for costs under that term, the seller is also obliged to pay duties and taxes on import. Should agreement be reached between the parties that certain of the import costs are excluded from the seller's obligations the wording may be suitably amended. For example 'Delivered Duty Paid, VAT Unpaid'.

We all appreciate updating of information materials and

Incoterms 1990 has made a number of useful additions and amendments to earlier editions. Although the use of electronic data interchange (EDI) has not increased to the extent envisaged by its most fervent supporters, it is now a significant factor in relation to the documentation supporting the international movement of goods. This has been recognized in the new edition. As regards costs and charges incurred in obtaining *documents* and their division between seller and buyer, the new terms make clear that the provisions apply equally to 'equivalent electronic messages'. The mode of transport for many movements of goods has altered significantly and multimodal journeys are more frequent. As a result the term *FCA Free Carrier* is intended to apply in situations where any mode of transport including multimodal is being employed, and the previously used terms specific to stated forms of transport, that is FOB Airport (FOA) and Free on Rail/Free on Truck (FOR/FOT), have been discontinued. To avoid misunderstandings and consequential risks of loss the correct term for the intended transport mode must be used and the following guide is of assistance:

Delivery Term	Mode of Transport
EXW FCA* CPT CIP DAF DDU DDP	Any, including Multimodal
FAS FOB CFR CIF DES DEQ	Sea and Inland Waterway

*FCA is the normal delivery term when the seller is responsible for delivery of goods to a carrier for transport by air or rail at the expense of the buyer.

Calculation of the Quoted Export Price

The **ladder** form of illustrating the relationship between individual costs and delivery terms – that is building up the costs to be included from the minimal list appropriate to 'ex works' step by step to the maximum list appropriate to 'delivered duty paid', serves to clarify the process of compiling the price.

Transport Mode	Costs to be included	Delivery term/ price
Any Mode	Raw materials and components Labour Manufacturing costs Additions specific to order Overheads Profit margin	
		Ex Works £
Any Mode	**Plus** Inland transport to port of shipment/carrier's premises Documentation costs and customs costs/duties payable on exportation Finance and credit term charges Credit insurance costs Sundries – postage, telex, EDI	
		FAS £ or FCA

	Plus	
By Sea	Charges incurred in port handling	

FOB £

	Plus	
Any Mode	Carriage contract charges (for example, freight)	

CFR £
or CPT

	Plus	
By Sea	Insurance	

CIF £
or CIP

Plus

Any Mode — Unloading charges at port of destination (if by sea); Cost of customs formalities and other import charges; Warehouse and transportation in buyer's country; Import duties and taxes

DDP £

To return to our example, an understanding of delivery terms added to that of the elements of basic price should enable PDB Exports (93) Ltd to identify the nature of costs to be included in their quotation to Relay Reactions Inc., but the following questions remain in determining policy and choosing between the options in arriving at final figures:

1 How dependable in terms of regular supply and price are suppliers of raw materials and components?

2 What considerations should be borne in mind in assessing the profit margin?

3 Should credit terms be offered and, if so, what should be their duration?

4 Which delivery term is most appropriate to the individual circumstances of the enquiry?

5 Should the final price be expressed in sterling or the currency of the buyer's country, such as Canadian dollars?

In examining the answers to these questions we are immediately face to face with two of the most important realities of international trade. The first, familiar to any experienced exporter, is that the aims of seller and buyer are opposed at the outset of negotiations as the following list illustrates.

Seller's Aims	Buyer's Aims
As high a profit margin as possible	As inexpensive a purchase as possible
As short a credit period as possible (or preferably cash terms and ideally an advance payment)	As long a credit period as possible
Delivery terms which are the least onerous to the seller	Delivery terms which are the least onerous to the buyer
Pricing in the currency of the seller's country	Pricing in the currency of the buyer's country

The second reality is that a compromise must be sought and, a fact that is frequently overlooked by the casual or inexperienced exporter, the ideal agreement is one in which both seller and buyer feel they have secured a fair deal. On this basis is created a worthwhile and profitable relationship which will never result from a single transaction in which one or the other is clearly seen to have been disadvantaged.

Profit Margin, Pricing Policy and Delivery Terms

In surveying a market the exporter will have in mind the basic price and on-costs dependent on the delivery term applied. These represent the expenses which must be recoverable. The margin between these expenses and the amount which can reasonably be expected in payment is the profit to the exporter. That margin will vary from market to market including the domestic market where profit margins may or may not be below those on export sales. Any given overseas country to which an exporter is selling may be a buyer's market – the supply of its particular goods exceeds demand – or a seller's market in which the demand for its particular product exceeds the supply. Naturally profit margins obtainable in a seller's market exceed those available in a buyer's market.

Coupled with the balance between demand and supply is the question of the elasticity of the former by which we mean the demand likely to be generated if supply increases. For example capital goods of a type where most households already have the appliance are likely to have an inelastic demand whereas consumer goods may have a considerable capacity for additional sales at the right price – demand may be described as elastic. The number of suppliers competing to fulfil an existing demand, be it elastic or inelastic, is also vital to a would-be exporter's research on price levels and profit margins; competition intensity is a prime influence.

In our example PDB Exports may well have discovered through market research the level of price at which Relay Reactions, as importers and end users, are likely to be buyers; if not the response to the quotation will probably reveal this information.

A different situation on price exists when the importer is a distributor or agent who is on-selling to the ultimate buyer. In this case significant increases will be made to the exporter's price by the importer in order to fix that at which the goods will be sold to the ultimate buyer. The exporter's interest in this final price lies in its effect on that which the importer is prepared to pay; if there is insufficient profit in the on-sale, the importer will not be prepared to do business. To illustrate the often considerable on-costs let us change our example to a sale by PDB Exports of scarves to a distributor in North America, where it is common for distributors to work in terms of discounts from retail price. The calculation might therefore appear as follows.

The retail price of a scarf is	$12.00

To sell at this retail price the retailer takes
a mark-up of 50% on the **retail** price ($6.00)
and therefore expects to buy from the distributor at $6.00

The distributor operates on a 20% margin (mark-up) on the price to the **retailer** ($1.20) and
therefore expects to buy from the exporter at
a delivered price of $4.80

Thus the exporter must allow in his calculations for a delivered price no higher than $4.80 if the retail shop price in the United States is $12.00. Although mark-ups may vary in amount and may sometimes be calculated on the above pattern and on other occasions as a percentage build-up on the imported price, the steep increase from import to retail sale is common to both as is shown by a similar example of a notional mark-up on a sale to Italy.

CIP Rome	2,000,000 Lira
TVA (8%)	160,000 Lira
Warehouse charges and inland transport	40,000 Lira
Distributor's total expenses	2,200,000 Lira
Mark-up on sale to retail outlet (12%)	264,000 Lira
Distributors price to retailer	2,464,000 Lira
Retailer's mark-up (45%)	1,108,800 Lira
Price to consumer	3,372,800 Lira

The use of a distributor is characterized by the need for the exporter to conduct additional research in order to ascertain prices in the market place and this is often achieved by an on-the-spot survey or by retail price lists obtainable through various sources. We will now look at a reverse situation, where the exporter is contributing to the United Kingdom export effort but through a sale made on a purely domestic basis involving the minimum of complications usually attributed to selling overseas, an important consideration for the company inexperienced in such matters.

Three types of purchasers buy in the United Kingdom in order to supply the overseas markets: export merchants, confirming houses and buying offices for large stores abroad.

Export merchants

The percentage of British export trade dealt with by export merchants has declined considerably over the years, but the volume is still substantial and these companies offer a valuable service, particularly to the small manufacturer who may lack the in-house expertise to develop overseas potential for their goods and where the anticipated volumes may be insufficient to warrant creating an export department. The merchant may have a general business seeking markets for a wide variety of exportable products or may specialize in marketing particular ranges. Thus some manufacturers may seek a merchant to buy all their potential exports while others may include the merchant as one of a number of outlets but with special emphasis on a limited range of products.

From the small manufacturer's viewpoint the attraction of using a merchant is that the sale is made on the least onerous delivery terms (usually Ex-Works but on occasion FCA, FAS or FOB) and payment is against invoice with essentially domestic market documentation. Export merchants purchase for their own account.

Confirming houses

These intermediaries in internal trade purchase from United Kingdom manufacturers for account of principals resident in the overseas markets, frequently but not always distributors. Some confirming houses have long-established connections with particular overseas countries, often originating in the Empire era but continuing under Commonwealth arrangements; a large proportion of their orders emanate from principals in the Less Developed Countries. Houses operate on a commission basis and quite frequently seek suppliers of a wide range of products destined for a collective project in the overseas market. As with export merchants the confirming houses make life simpler for the small manufacturer than it would be with direct exporting, prices normally being quoted FOB leaving the house to wrestle with questions of transportation, insurance and import formalities.

Buying offices

Concentrating on the consumer goods market, a number of buying offices in the United Kingdom (mainly London) represent major overseas departmental stores. Their function is not dissimilar to that of a confirming house in that they act on behalf of a foreign principal but the buying office's activities are confined to the retail group or groups they represent. Purchases are made across a broad range of goods and, contrary to reports sometimes heard, the amount purchased can vary from modest to very large orders. The goods are delivered within the United Kingdom and, once more, the supplier is excused most of the complexities of documentation.

Credit Terms

Competition is as strong a force in determining credit terms as it is in influencing which delivery term is agreed. However an important difference to us in our consideration of payment is that while a choice of the wrong delivery term, perhaps involving the seller in formalities with which it is unfamiliar or ill-equipped to handle, may prejudice the efficient performance of contract; unwise extension of credit, both as regards amount and duration, is likely to result in delay or default in payment.

This will moreover occur irrespective of how efficiently the exporter has performed his obligations under the contract.

It is normally relatively simple for the exporter through trade enquiries to ascertain the customary credit terms offered to the average buyer in a major market. Where prudence is necessary is in the variations which the exporter might allow, or should insist on, from that average. As observed in chapter 2, credit terms are an important part of buyer risk, and replies to status enquiries should be carefully read before the decision on any particular enquiry is made. The method of payment is also relevant as the security it provides might minimize the risk inherent in giving credit, and finally the advisability of credit insurance should receive consideration.

Foreign Exchange Pricing

The answer to the question of whether the price quoted to the buyer should be in the seller's or the buyer's currency requires an understanding by the exporter of foreign exchange, a subject which many find difficult to understand. It is examined in the following chapter.

4

Foreign Exchange

Of the many colleagues I have worked with over the years two in particular come to mind when thinking about foreign exchange and the exporter. The first, who was both an astute banker and an accomplished speaker, used to start his talk to those about to venture into overseas markets with the words 'there are three reasons for exporting – profit, profit and profit'. In this unusual introduction Ray was not encouraging his audience's greed but seeking to ensure that at each stage in the life cycle of an export they kept firmly in mind that the object was to avoid loss. He would follow, as we are attempting in this book, by examining the inherent risks and advising how each should be avoided or minimized to keep one's profit margin intact. Implicit in the advice is the need for thought before action.

The second colleague, who also possessed many talents, held the view that a measure of one's ability was the degree to which immediate enthusiasm and action were applied to any task, and eyed suspiciously any sign of hesitancy pending examination of problems faced. In relation to the risks of foreign exchange I cannot have any doubt that the time taken in preparation is well spent and an impetuous approach can be an expensive folly.

Convertibility of Currencies

'Convertibility' is a term used to describe the facility with which a currency can be converted into another by a holder, at any one time, through a sale on a recognized foreign exchange market. More simply, if you or I as exporters receive such a currency in payment, are we able to request our bank to purchase it against sterling to ensure that it is credited to our account, or even to purchase it against a third currency (say) United States dollars to be credited to an account in the United States? If the answer is an unqualified 'yes' then the currency we have received is 'fully convertible', one of the three classifications into which all world currencies fall; the others being 'limited convertibility' and 'non-convertible'.

Correctly classifying any currency suggested by a buyer for payment is the first essential in deciding if the suggestion should be seriously considered. A non-convertible currency accepted as settlement by an enthusiastic salesman is unlikely to endear him to the managing director. It would be an exaggeration to say that a non-convertible currency is useless to an exporter but the purposes for which it is usable are strictly limited and normally confined to such internal payments as may be permitted by the authorities of the country in question. The expenses incurred during a sales trip might well qualify for permission and in some instances it is possible to use funds to make a direct investment such as a joint venture with a local company or the establishment of manufacturing capacity. In other cases, direct investments are approved only if the funds are remitted from the investor's country thus providing valuable foreign exchange. Whatever limited opportunities exist for usage, however, the acceptance of a 'non-convertible' currency is never satisfactory if convertibility was expected and would have been the criterion in deciding whether or not to agree to settlement in currency. Although many currencies are well-known to exporters as not being convertible, this is not always the case and circumstances change; if in doubt consult your bank.

While not as serious in its repercussions as accepting a non-convertible currency a decision to accept one which has limited convertibility is unwise, with the possible exception of the experienced exporter who has taken professional advice. Limited convertibility means that one or more restrictions exist on full convertibility. The currency may only be quoted in a limited number of foreign exchange markets, perhaps at a discount, the market may be thin (only a few firms or individuals are prepared to deal) and the exchange rate consequently unrepresentative of value, or the amounts of the currency in which the market is prepared to deal are restricted. Only a spot market (see later in this chapter) may exist, or the rate of exchange at which deals may be affected is determined by the authorities in the country concerned, and conversion is therefore only possible in that country and at a rate of exchange which bears little relation to what the rate would be if normal forces of demand and supply were in operation as in a normal foreign exchange market.

Quoting in Currency

Assuming that an exporter through experience, or seeking banker's advice, avoids the risk of accepting non-convertible or limited convertibility currency, what would be considered in deciding whether to quote in a convertible currency or in sterling? If an exporter quotes in sterling the amount receivable on settlement is payable in sterling: it matters not to the exporter if a greater amount of the buyer's currency is necessary to acquire the sterling amount **on the date of settlement** than would have been required **when the quotation was received by the buyer**. No claim for any such difference can therefore be made by the buyer to the exporter.

Conversely if an exporter quotes in the currency of the buyer's country it is the amount in that currency which is receivable on settlement. It matters not to the buyer if that amount produces a smaller amount in sterling when converted on the date of settlement than it would have produced on the date the quotation was made. No claim for any such difference can therefore be made from the exporter to the buyer.

The Exchange Risk

It is clear from the above that an exchange risk lies in the possibility of exchange rates between the currencies of the exporters' and buyers' countries moving adversely between the date of quotation and the date of settlement. The risk will always be present, but a decision about whether it will be carried by the exporter or the buyer will depend on the currency of quotation (and invoice). To illustrate, envisage PDB Exports (93) Ltd having the option to quote to Relay Reactions Inc. of Toronto in either £ sterling or Canadian dollars for the supply of 15,000 widgets and that the cost, insurance and freight price of £20,000, calculated on the basis explained in chapter 3, includes a profit margin of £5,000 (33.33 per cent). Between the quotation and payment dates the exchange rates (ignoring the spread between buying and selling rates) move as follows:

quotation date: £1 = Can$1.8220
payment date: £1 = Can$2.1500

What effect does this change have on the exporter and the buyer respectively where the quotation is (A) £ sterling or (B) Canadian dollars?

(A) The exporter still receives £20,000 and the profit margin is unchanged The buyer, had the quoted price of £20,000 been purchased on the quotation date, would have paid $1.8220 x 20,000 = Can$36,440.

However to acquire £20,000 on the payment date would have cost $2.1500 x 20,000, Can$43,000, an increase of Can$6,560. Thus the buyer has suffered an increase in cost and if on-selling this would lower the profit margin accordingly.

(B) The buyer still pays $36,440 (assuming the exporter based the Canadian dollar quotation on the rate of exchange at that time) and if on-selling the profit margin is unchanged. Had the exporter sold Can$36,440 on the quotation date, $36,440 divided by 1.8220 = £20,000, would have been received.

However the sale of the same amount of dollars on the payment date would have yielded $36,440 divided by 2.1500 = £16,948, a decrease of £3,052. Thus the exporter has suffered a decrease in receipts reducing the profit margin from 33.33 per cent to 20.33 per cent.

Although the concern of the parties relates to the possibility of exchange rate movements causing a loss, it is equally possible that they may result in a profit. The principle is however the same; the party which will benefit from the profit will depend on the currency of quotation. If we rework the above example with the same assumptions except that the rates of exchange move as follows the principle will be apparent. Quotation date: £1 = Can$1.8220, payment date: £1 = Can$1.5250. In the case of (A), the exporter still receives £20,000 and the profit margin is unchanged. The buyer, had the quoted price of £20,000 been purchased against Canadian dollars on the quotation date, would have paid $1,8220 x 20,000 = Can$36,440. However to acquire £20,000 on the payment date would have cost $1.5250 x 20,000 = Can$30,500, a saving of Can$5,940. Thus the buyer, if on-selling, would have improved the profit margin.

In the case of (B), the buyer will still pay Can$36,440 (assuming the exporter based the Canadian dollar quotation on the rate of exchange at that time) and if on-selling will have an unchanged profit margin.

By selling Can$36,440 on the quotation date the exporter would have received $36,440 divided by 1.8220 = £20,000. However the sale of the same amount of dollars on the payment date would have yielded $36,440 divided by 1.5250 = £23,895, an increase of £3,895. Thus the exporter has increased receipts and raised the profit margin from 33.33 per cent to 59.25 per cent.

Changes in exchange rates over the period from quotation to settlement are of equal concern to importers who may find their costs increased if imports are invoiced in currency and an adverse movement in rates occurs. The principle that a quotation in sterling will protect the United Kingdom party against exchange risk is as valid for imports as for exports, the risk being transferred to the seller. Why then, if both exporters and importers in the United Kingdom are protected from exchange risk by dealing in sterling invoicing, is this not invariably the best course of action?

Yet again we return to our reminder of realism and not theory; competition. In a seller's market United Kingdom exporters might well be advised to adopt sterling invoicing as an invariable rule, but in a buyer's market competitors will be prepared to invoice in the currency of the buyer's country. In so doing they will not only be removing the exchange risk as an inducement to buy but will serve the buyer's convenience in enabling the calculation of on-selling prices over a period. Similarly United Kingdom importers may well ask for quotations in sterling in a buyer's market but could experience difficulty in obtaining supplies on that basis were this to change to a seller's market.

On occasion exports may be quoted in the buyer's currency but with a clause inserted tying the amount to a fixed rate of exchange against sterling. While this may be satisfactory when dealings are between parties who understand the implication, to permit adjustments if the rate of exchange alters, experience suggests the practice should be used sparingly as it often involves disputes due to misunderstanding particularly among unsophisticated exporters.

Before turning to the question of understanding how rates of exchange are published and what precautions can be taken to minimize exchange risk, consider the argument sometimes advanced that since movements in rates can as often be to the advantage of the exporter as to its disadvantage, is it not better to disregard the exchange risk? This swings and roundabouts viewpoint is perhaps comparable to that of calling a coin – it will as often fall tails as heads; over an extended period that may be true but on every single occasion the chance is 50 per cent. Is the exporter in business to speculate? As my friend Ray warned, lose sight of profit at your peril; speculation will place that profit in jeopardy. The business of an exporter is to sell goods and that in itself involves sufficient risks without seeking to indulge in currency speculation.

Understanding Rates of Exchange

Considerable sums of money are lost every year by exporters due to a misreading of rates of exchange. Instructions given to banks are sincerely believed to be to sell currency when they are, in fact, to buy or calculations in converting prices from sterling into currency are based on the wrong rates. Examine the rates as they appear in the press daily and endeavour to clarify some of the main areas which give rise to errors.

Exhibit 4.1: London Foreign Exchange Market – Sterling Spot Rates of Exchange

Country	X February 19XX Rates	Previous Close
Austria	16.65 – 16.70	16.50 – 16.55
Belgium	48.96 – 49.06	48.32 – 48.44
Canada	1.8210 – 1.8231	1.8197 – 1.8218
Denmark	9.0580 – 9.0790	8.9820 – 9.0040
France	8.0090 – 8.0220	7.9110 – 7.9240
Germany	2.3629 – 2.3661	2.3448 – 2.3480
Holland	2.6653 – 2.6702	2.6418 – 2.6452
Ireland	0.9470 – 0.9610	0.9650 – 0.9790
Italy	2254.00 – 2261.00	2226.50 – 2231.00
Japan	172.67 – 172.87	172.43 – 172.71
Norway	10.0400 – 10.0630	9.9800 – 10.0020
Portugal	216.03 – 216.92	214.79 – 215.23
Spain	171.03 – 171.88	168.83 – 169.10
Sweden	10.9300 – 10.9530	10.7210 – 10.7440
Switzerland	2.1849 – 2.1880	2.1656 – 2.1686
United States	1.4470 – 1.4480	1.4430 – 1.4440
ECU	1.2215 – 1.2273	1.2047 – 1.2103

Notes: For simplicity this table is confined to spot rates. However spot and forward rates are usually amalgamated in published quotations.

The published lists normally include all fully convertible currencies but in times of extreme volability the market may omit the currencies affected.

When currencies are sold for immediate delivery to the bank (immediate means within two working days) against sterling or purchased for immediate delivery through a payment in sterling the deal is said to be effected in the spot market and a spot rate of exchange is applied. In the export context such a deal would take place if the exporter awaits payment from the buyer on the due date for an export invoiced in currency and upon receipt sells that currency to the bank in the spot market. A complete set of spot rates will be found in exhibit 4.1 indicating the range of currencies quoted.

In exhibit 4.1 rates are quoted in pairs; the left hand figure being that at which the bank will sell the currency, the right hand that at which the bank will purchase the currency. An easy way to remember the correct figure to apply is that the **bank** buys high and sells low. Thus an exporter selling goods to Germany against settlement in deutschmarks will upon receipt of proceeds request its bank to purchase them, crediting the sterling sum to its account. The bank will buy at 2.3661, the right hand and highest figure in the pair quoted.

An importer wishing to buy deutschmarks from the bank in order to pay for goods imported from a German seller will however receive the currency at 2.3629, the rate applied by the bank in selling, the left hand and lowest figure in the pair quoted. It is also important to remember that a purchase of currency by the bank is a sale by their customer and conversely a sale by the bank is a purchase by their customer. Obvious? Perhaps, but worth stressing as in the giving and receiving of orders to buy or sell it is so easy for a slight error to result in the opposite deal to that intended, for instance a purchase instead of a sale. As will be seen from the mock confirmation by a bank's foreign exchange dealers to the instructing branch of a deal, reproduced in exhibit 4.2, great care is taken to make clear who is purchasing and who is selling the currency but the issue of that document is, of course, after the deal has been effected and any mistakes made between branch and customer.

Since banks cover their own risk in buying or selling currency by a corresponding deal in the inter-bank market, thus balancing the books, it is also true that if an error has occurred this will involve expense in reversing the transaction; the cost is charged to the customer if the mistake was theirs. These errors became sufficiently frequent in recent years that many banks in preference, or in addition, to the use of the type of confirmation in exhibit 4.2, now record the giving and receipt of instructions for foreign exchange deals where these are by telephone.

Exhibit 4.2: Specimen Forward Exchange Contract Confirmation

Hampshire County Bank plc

TO: Anytown Branch

FROM: Forex Division
Lombard Court
Major Town

Forward Exchange Contract Dated 12th June 19XX

Account   Little Gem Export Inc.

We confirm that Hampshire County Bank has PURCHASED from your customer: German Marks 50,000 @ 2.55665

FOR DELIVERY 12th July 19XX

Sterling Equivalent £19,556.84

These details should be checked immediately and the attached duplicate copy of this advice returned by way of confirmation. In the event of any discrepancy immediate notification should be made to The Manager, Forex Division quoting our reference FEC 1246.

Failure to effect delivery on the agreed date could result in a charge to your customer and to avoid delays advice of settlement should be in our hands 48 hours (2 working days) before the 12th July 19XX. The Sterling equivalent will be paid to you against delivery of the currency.

PLEASE NOTE that under this contract your customer has agreed to SELL German Marks to Hampshire County Bank.

The triplicate copy of this advice is intended to be sent by you to your customer.

The rates quoted in our exhibit are those at which the bank will sell or buy a currency against £1 sterling. They are in this instance, but not in all rates of exchange, quoted in decimals. In the case of currencies where a substantial number of units of the currency are equivalent to £1 sterling (for example the Italian lira quoted at 2254 – 2261), the quotations are usually in whole numbers only, whereas in instances where the number of units equivalent to £1 sterling are relatively low, quotations will be given to two or four decimal places.

An indication is also given in the spot market of the rates quoted at the previous close. As newspapers publish the rates at which currencies were bought and sold at the close of business yesterday, the previous close figures will be those at the end of business on the day before yesterday. The purpose of including these latter figures is to indicate any trend which may be apparent which is not ascertainable from a single set of rates.

A final observation on the exhibit: the difference between the rate at which a bank sells a currency and that at which it buys the same currency is termed the spread and constitutes the bank's profit in dealing. This is a significant consideration when assessing the position of internationally trading companies who both import and export, in consequence, buying and selling the same currency.

You will have noticed that our exhibit does not cover all the currencies which we might have expected to be quoted in London. The market does however quote indication rates for various other currencies, some of which may have limited convertibility, and a typical list appears in exhibit 4.3.

Forward Exchange Contracts

Our review of spot rates of exchange may have helped to avoid some of the misunderstanding which occurs in selling and buying currencies, and in the interpretation of published rates; but it does not help in combating the exchange risk. As long as currencies are purchased or sold in the spot market as they are required to settle an import bill or received in payment for an export invoiced in the currency concerned, then the importer or exporter will be at risk from exchange rate movements over the period from quotation or order to settlement.

To enable the exchange risk to be covered, foreign exchange markets are prepared to deal forward in convertible currencies and banks will enter into forward exchange contracts with exporters or importers. A forward exchange contract involves the bank in a commitment to purchase or sell currency, at a rate of exchange agreed at the time of entering into the contract, for delivery at a fixed future date or between two fixed dates in the future. The exporter entering into a forward contract at the commencement of a sale where invoicing is to be in the buyer's currency can therefore fix the amount in sterling which will be received when payment in currency is delivered to the bank.

Exhibit 4.3: London Foreign Exchange Market – Other Market Rates against Sterling

	X February 19XX
Argentine Peso	1.4402
Australian Dollar	2.1077
Brazilian Cruzeiro	27196.0
Cyprus Pound	0.7037
Finland Markka	8.4090
Greek Drachma	317.07
Hong Kong Dollar	11.1410
Indian Rupee	42.6894
Kuwait Dinar	0.9540
Malaysian Ringgit	3.7880
Pakistan Rupee	37.25
Saudi Arabian Ryal	5.3875
Singapore Dollar	2.3650
South African Rand	6.6950
Taiwan Dollar	37.43
United Arab Emirates Dirham	5.2775

There are two types of foreign exchange forward contracts; fixed and option. A fixed contract specifies the future date upon which delivery is to be made to the bank and is appropriate when the date of payment for the export is reasonably predictable. An option contract specifies two dates between which delivery is to be made, for example one and two months from the date of the contract and affords valuable flexibility in those cases where the date of payment for the export is less easily predictable. Exporters must not confuse a foreign exchange forward option with a stock exchange option; while the latter gives the ability to walk away if delivery is not seen to be in the holder's best interests, the former provides only an option in time of delivery which must be made as a contractual obligation.

The firm obligation to deliver under a forward exchange contract whether fixed or option is also relevant to the point of time when an exporter will choose to contract with the bank. There is no technical reason why a contract should not be concluded when a quotation for the sale of goods is sent by the exporter to the potential buyer and this will obviously give immediate protection to the profit margin. Should the potential buyer decide not to purchase then the exporter has the obligation to deliver currency to the bank at the time agreed and must make arrangements to do so notwithstanding no longer being able to expect the sum from the would-be buyer. The methods of closing out the forward contract in these circumstances will be discussed later in this chapter when it will be seen that a loss to the exporter could arise.

It is therefore desirable for an exporter to cover forward at the time of quotation for the sale of goods only when it is virtually certain that the quotation will be accepted (in some cases of continuing business the quotation may be little more than a formality). If that degree of certainty is not present, it is preferable to allow a slight adjustment to the exchange rate used to calculate the currency quotation in order to give a small hedge against adverse movements between quotation and acceptance, but to defer covering forward until that acceptance is to hand.

Forward Exchange Rates

The national press publishes daily rates of exchange on the London Foreign Exchange Market for forward contracts.

Although the published rates are normally confined to those applicable for one month and three month forward deals, corresponding with export sales on 30 or 90 day terms, the London market is one of the most sophisticated in the world and prides itself on being able, upon request, to quote forward for a wide variety of periods, including split dates, those not involving complete calendar periods (months or weeks).

The following is an extract from a typical table of forward rates as they might appear in the press; a complete set indicating the wide range of currencies quoted appears in exhibit 4.4.

Currency	One month	Three months
Austria	1¾-2¾ Gr Discount	3¼-5 Gr Discount
Canada	0.09-0.03 c.Premium	0.15-0.03 c.Premium
France	3¼-3⅞ c.Discount	10⅝-11⅝ c.Discount
Germany	⅜-½ Pfg.Discount	1¼-1⅜ Pfg.Discount
Italy	8-10 Lr Discount	27-30 Lr Discount
Switzerland	¼-⅛ c.Premium	⅜-¼ c.Premium
United States	0.35-0.33 c.Premium	1.06-1.04 c.Premium

The forward rates appear as adjustments that are made to the spot rates producing the figure at which the bank will sell or purchase the currency forward. Again the groupings are in pairs and follow the same rule as for spot rates: the left hand figure is the adjustment to be made to the spot rate at which the bank sells the currency; the right hand figure is the adjustment required to the bank's buying rate. The forward rates are generally expressed in the minor unit of currency of the country, unlike spot rates which quote the major unit; for example, the United States spot rate is expressed in dollars, but the forward rate in cents. Exceptions among the rates normally published are Italy and Japan where both spot and forward rates are in lira and yen respectively.

Each quotation shows as a suffix, dis or pm, which stand for discount and premium respectively. A discount shows that the market anticipates a depreciation in the value of the currency against sterling over the future period quoted whereas a premium indicates that an appreciation against sterling is anticipated for the period in question. Although it does not appear in the list there is a third category, par, which indicates that no change in value against sterling is envisaged over the future period.

Exhibit 4.4: London Foreign Exchange Market – Sterling Forward Rates of Exchange

Country	One Month		Three Months	
	X February 19XX			
Austria	1.75 – 2.75	Gr dis	3.25 – 5	Gr dis
Belgium	11 – 15	c dis	32 – 38	c dis
Canada	0.09 – 0.03	c pm	0.15 – 0.03	c pm
Denmark	7 – 12.25	Ore dis	24.625 – 33.50	Ore dis
France	3.25 – 3.875	c dis	10.625 – 11.625	c dis
Germany	.375 – .50	Pfg dis	1.25 – 1.375	Pfg dis
Holland	.375 – .50	c dis	1.125 – .50	c dis
Italy	8 – 10	Lr dis	27 – 30	Lr dis
Japan	.25 – .375	Yen pm	1.375 – 1.125	Yen pm
Norway	1.125 – 3	Ore dis	5.625 – 8	Ore dis
Portugal	119 – 128	c dis	365 – 391	c dis
Spain	94 – 111	c dis	301 – 326	c dis
Sweden	1.625 – 3.875	Ore dis	6.50 – 8.875	Ore dis
Switzerland	.25 – .125	c dis	.375 – .25	c pm
United States	0.35 – 0.33	c pm	1.06 – 1.04	c pm

Notes: For simplicity this table is confined to forward rates and a separate table of spot rates appears in Exhibit 4.1. However the two are usually amalgamated in published quotations.

The published lists normally include all fully convertible currencies but in times of extreme volatility the market may omit the currencies affected.

Contrary to the belief sometimes voiced, in calculating forward rates bankers do not rely on a crystal ball! The main influence on the discounts and premiums is the relative interest rates between the countries concerned; for example, if sterling interest rates are below those for United States dollars, the dollar is likely to be at a forward discount against sterling.

If however dollar interest rates are below those for sterling then the United States dollar is likely to be at a forward premium against sterling. This interrelation between forward foreign exchange and interest rates may seem strange at first, but is easily appreciated if we understand how the bank buying currency forward from an exporter operates.

Any single foreign exchange deal with a customer is probably negligible in size compared with the bank's resources and the risk in dealing is therefore very small. Imagine however the cumulative amount of deals done in any one day by one of the clearing banks and the position is vastly different: huge sums are involved. In its own interests the banks would not wish to run the major risk of leaving its position uncovered in the event of exchange rate movements and additionally there is an indirect national interest in the exposure.

To hedge the risk the bank borrows an amount in the currency which it has agreed to purchase forward from exporters (say United States dollars) in 90 days' time and sells the proceeds of the loan against sterling. The sterling received is then invested in the London market for the 90-day period. When that period is complete the sterling is paid to the exporters and the dollars they deliver under the terms of the forward contracts are used by the bank to repay the loan it took at the commencement of the period.

Thus the bank has covered its risk and in so doing has incurred a cost represented by the interest rate on the dollars it borrowed against which it offsets the interest earned on the sterling it deposited. If the latter exceeds the former, that is, London interest rates are higher than those in New York, the differential is passed on to exporters in the premium reflected in the forward contract rate; if the converse applies, when New York interest rates exceed those in London, the differential is claimed from exporters in the discount reflected in the forward contract rate.

Calculating Forward Exchange Rates

Using the spot rates of exchange and the forward rates for the same currencies as previously quoted the following four calculations show typical quotations which will be made by the bank to the exporter or importer for fixed forward contracts.

1 50,000 Canadian dollars sold forward by the exporter to the bank for delivery in three months' time. Spot rate at which the bank buys Canadian dollars: 1.8231 (to the £1). (Note the right hand figure in the pair quoted is used). Subtract the forward premium .0003. (Note premiums are always subtracted from the spot rate). The bank will quote 1.8228 (to the £1).

In this case the exporter will receive a greater amount of sterling by selling forward than would have been produced by a spot conversion of the dollars (50,000 divided by 1.8231 = £27,425, 50,000 divided by 1.8228 = £27,430) and has eliminated the exchange risk.

2 100,000 deutschmarks sold forward by the exporter to the bank for delivery in one month's time. Spot rate at which the bank buys deutschmarks: 2.3661 (to the £1). (Note the right hand figure in the pair quoted is used). Add the forward discount .0050. (Note discounts are always added to the spot rate). The bank will quote 2.3711 (to the £1).

Thus the exporter will receive a smaller amount of sterling by selling forward than would have been produced by a spot conversion of the deutschmarks (100,000 divided by 2.3661 = £42,263, 100,000 divided by 2.3711 = £42,174) but has eliminated the exchange risk.

3 200,000 French francs purchased forward by an importer from the bank for delivery in one month's time. Spot rate at which the bank sells French francs: 8.0090 (to the £1). (Note the left hand figure in the pair quoted is used). Add the forward discount .0325. The bank will quote 8.0415 (to the £1).

Thus the importer will receive a greater amount of currency for sterling than would have been received by a spot conversion (200,000 francs divided by 8.0415 = £24,870, 200,000 francs divided by 8.0090 = £24,971) and has eliminated the exchange risk.

4 50,000 Swiss francs purchased forward by an importer from the bank for delivery in three months' time. Spot rate at which the bank sells Swiss francs: 2.1849 (to the £1). (Note the left hand figure in the pair quoted is used). Subtract the forward premium .00375. The bank will quote 2.18115 (to the £1).

Thus the importer will receive a smaller amount of currency for sterling than would have been received by a spot conversion (50,000 francs divided by 2.18165 = £22,918, 50,000 francs divided by 2.1849 = £22,884) but has eliminated the exchange risk.

Before leaving these examples three important points should be made.

The practice of quoting forward rates in either decimals or fractions can cause confusion. In the forward quote the fraction or decimal is of the minor unit of the currency and care must be taken that it is correctly positioned in making the addition or subtraction. In example 2 the spot rate of 2.3661 could be expressed as 2 deutschmarks 36.61 pfennigs and the premium is $1/2$ or .50 of a pfennig: therefore in the calculation it appears as .0050.

Although for simplicity the results of a sale or purchase have been compared at a forward rate with those of a sale or purchase at the spot rate on the same day and described the benefit or cost to the exporter or importer, this is not a true comparison. At the date of the forward contract we do not know the spot rate which will apply **on the date delivery is made** and it is that rate which will determine if the exporter or importer has received a monetary advantage from covering forward. What is certain, however, is that by so doing the profit margin included in the quotation has been protected notwithstanding any adverse movement in the spot rate, and anxiety has been avoided.

When a foreign exchange forward option contract is concluded the rate which the bank quotes is that which is best from its own point of view. Assume an exporter desires to sell Deutschmarks forward to the bank for delivery at any time between the contract date and three months thereafter, that is, option 3 months forward. The rates published are: Spot: 2.3661 (per £1), Add 3 months forward discount .01375, 3 months forward rate 2.37985 (per £1).

Should the bank quote the spot rate or that for 3 months forward? The answer is it will quote the 3 months forward rate as this will give 2.37985 deutschmarks for every £1 paid out, whereas only 2.3661 would be received for each £1 were the spot rate used.

If, however, the bank had been selling deutschmarks to an importer with a similar option, the position would have been somewhat different; the published rates being: Spot: 2.3629 (per £1), Add 3 months forward discount .0125, 3 months forward rate 2.3754 (per £1).

In this case the bank would have quoted the spot rate as this will require it to deliver only 2.3629 deutschmarks for each £1 compared with 2.3754 for each £1 if the 3 months forward rate were quoted.

The principle is identical for currencies quoted at a premium forward; the rate most advantageous to the bank (and least favourable to the customer) will be quoted in order that whenever delivery takes place within the permitted option the bank cannot lose.

Closing Out Forward Contracts

Despite an exporter taking the precaution of concluding an option forward contract if the date of payment of the goods is uncertain there may still be circumstances in which he cannot deliver the currency, for example a default by the buyer. In such a case the forward contract must be closed out, since, as already noted, the bank will have covered its risk through a compensating deal in the inter-bank market which it will have to honour. The way in which closing out is effected is by using the spot market.

Assume an exporter, which has sold Canadian dollars forward three months to the bank at a rate of 1.8228, discovers the deal with the Canadian customer has fallen through and, immediately prior to the delivery date for currency to the bank, advises it of the inability to complete. The bank will purchase the currency (say Can$50,000) in the spot market and apply the sum in completion of the forward contract. If the sterling used in the spot purchase exceeds that produced by completing the forward sale at the rate agreed when the forward contract was concluded, the exporter will be debited with the difference. If the sterling produced by the completed forward sale exceeds that required for the spot purchase, the difference will be credited to the exporter's account. No penal payment is requested by the bank on closure and the amount debited or credited to the customer is a straight reflection of the difference in spot and forward rates; references which are sometimes made to a penalty on closing out are therefore misleading.

If an exporter experiences a delay in payment for goods but not a default, it may request the bank to extend the forward contract. This will normally be arranged at a slightly more favourable rate to the exporter than would result were the existing contract to be closed out and a new forward contract concluded for the additional period required.

Closing out also illustrates that there is a liability from the customer to its bank in concluding a forward exchange contract; if the customer is unable to deliver the sterling or currency required for completion, the bank is left with an uncovered position on its compensating deal in the inter-bank market. As we have seen this involves a transaction in the spot market to rectify the position which, depending on the rates, may be expensive and a loss to the bank if its customer has become insolvent. For this reason banks may regard their willingness to deal forward with customers as part of the facilities made available to them and the risk is variously assessed at up to 100 per cent of the contract amount, although between 10-25 per cent is quite usual. The customer may also in certain cases be asked to make a cash deposit when concluding a contract.

Pure Currency Options

As already noted, foreign exchange forward contracts carry an obligation on the exporter to deliver currency on a fixed date or within specified time limits and provide no opportunity for it to walk away. The point has rightly been made that to cover forward protects profit, but it is also true that it deprives the exporter of the higher return that could have been gained if the spot rate moved appreciably in its favour between quotation for the export and settlement. This lack of flexibility has been resented by some international trading companies, particularly multinationals; in response to a perceived demand the foreign exchange market has introduced contracts known as **pure currency options** (or **true options** or **currency options**). Under this type of contract an exporter requests the bank to afford him the option to deliver at a fixed date, or within an agreed period, currency for exchange into sterling at a specified rate, known as the **strike price**. That price will normally be related to the profit margin built into the exporter's quotation to the buyer; the exporter will endeavour to pitch the strike price at the figure which was used to convert the (say) cash, insurance and freight price in sterling into currency or possibly a slightly higher or lower figure.

The pure currency option obliges the bank to accept the currency if tendered within the period (or by the date) agreed at the strike price or rate of exchange stated in the option, but, unlike a forward contract option, the exporter has only the right and not an obligation to deliver. The currency option also differs in that the exporter specifies the strike price or rate of exchange, not the bank. For this reason the bank's remuneration for the deal consists of a premium paid by the exporter when the pure currency option is arranged.

The amount of the premium depends on the strike price and the period during which it can be exercised. If the strike price specified by the exporter is outside market forward rates for the period, the premium will be high or, in extreme cases, prohibitive.

The Wider Picture

In this chapter we have so far concentrated on the ways in which those engaged in international trade can protect themselves against the exchange risk as it exists in world trading at present, firstly by ensuring convertibility of the currency offered in payment and secondly by concluding a contract with the bank. However it is recognized by governments that the exchange risk is a problem which is a national (or international) concern and it is interesting to observe some of the measures they have instituted in an endeavour to minimize fluctuations in rates and the success or lack of success of those measures.

To appreciate the extent of the problem, the factors influencing the demand for a particular currency must be considered. The most traditional calculation is enshrined in the **Purchasing Power Parity Theory** which states simply that the exchange rate between any two currencies will be determined by their relative purchasing power. Although this theory is more easily detectable in conditions which are not so volatile in terms of confidence and monetary policy as those today, it is still valid but obviously foreign exchange dealers do not engage in commercial market research before quoting exchange rates. It is the indicators of the economic health of a country, which will ultimately affect the purchasing power of its currency, that play a large part in influencing exchange rate movements.

The number of such indicators is considerable and they include inflation rates, interest rate differentials between countries, balance of payment statistics and housing starts, to name but a few; any one of these can cause rates to move. The imposition of exchange controls, international or internal unrest and political pronouncements play their part. Confidence in a currency can be a fragile commodity and the volume of commercial dealing, quite apart from non-commercial speculative deals, often acts as an accelerator to any movement. For example major companies in particular can, within limits, bring forward or defer their foreign exchange deals producing so called **leads** or **lags** which will increase the pressures towards significant rate changes.

What can governments acting in co-operation do nationally to mitigate the effects of exchange rate movements on trade, and indeed on their domestic economies? Readers will recall that in chapter 2 we examined one such initiative, that of the International Monetary Fund and the World Bank in seeking to assist countries experiencing balance of payments crises, to lessen the risk of these countries having to introduce measures involving competitive exchange devaluation and exchange controls. It would seem a fair judgment to comment that, although no action could prevent a monetary crisis in a country affecting international confidence and thus the value of its currency, the support of these organizations for the country concerned has certainly on occasion avoided the confidence crisis becoming a panic.

Another official attempt to create a system to limit exchange rate movements, this time in normal trading conditions as distinct from emergencies, was included in the Treaty of Rome which founded the European Economic Community (EEC). The European Monetary System (EMS) formed in 1979 is the present day method of implementing the desire to achieve full monetary co-operation, which was one of the stated aims of the treaty, and it follows an earlier system known as 'The Snake'. The principle underlying the snake was similar to that adopted following the Bretton Woods conference in 1944 resulting in a change to fixed exchange rates which were subsequently abandoned in 1972 with a return to floating rates. Each member of the European Monetary System agreed to a parity rate against the currencies of other members, and fluctuations from that parity were restricted to 2.25 per cent (except for the lira which was allowed a 6 per cent tolerance) at which point central bank intervention was obligatory to bring the currency back within the permitted band.

Exhibit 4.5: Make-up of the European Currency Unit (ECU) 1989 Review

Currency	Amount	Weighting %
Deutschmark	0.6242	30.5
French Franc	1.332	19.4
Sterling	0.08784	11.8
Lira	151.8	10.1
Guilder	0.2198	9.6
Belgian Franc	3.301	7.8
Peseta	6.885	5.3
Danish Kr	0.1976	2.5
Irish Pound	0.008552	1.1
Escudo	1.393	0.8
Drachma	1.44	0.7
Luxembourg Franc	0.13	0.3

The change in 1979 created the Exchange Rate Mechanism (ERM) within the European Monetary System which took over the snake but with important refinements. The most significant was to re-establish the parities (and permitted fluctuation bands) in terms of the European Currency Unit (ECU). The unit was also a brainchild of the system and is made up of a basket which includes all the 12 currencies of the countries currently in the Community. As the table in exhibit 4.5 illustrates the currencies are weighted within the ECU, the weighting based primarily on gross national product. The reasoning behind the change in relating individual parities to the ECU is that, since it is a basket of currencies not all of which are likely to move in the same direction or to the same extent at a given time, greater flexibility should be attained, and devaluations or revaluations of currencies should be less frequent.

The European Monetary System has retained the boundaries of the permitted exchange rate band under the snake, and there is an obligation for a member's central bank to intervene in foreign exchange markets should the currency reach 75 per cent of the maximum band divergence. In such intervention the central bank is supported by those of other member countries and short term finance arrangements are encouraged to assist in this co-operation. Further action may also be required from a member whose currency is threatening to breach the permitted exchange rate guidelines in the form of conventional monetary correctives, for example increases or decreases in interest rates. Allowance is made within the mechanism for realignment of currencies through changes in the parity rate but, as frequent alterations would be opposed to the principle of seeking greater stability, these have been made as rarely as possible.

To exporters and importers the implications of the creation of both the Exchange Rate Mechanism and the European Currency Unit are considerable and, if the desired stability can be achieved, favourable. The ECU is a currency which, for the first few years of its existence, was confined to an instrument for settling official transactions between members of the Community. So much was this the case that it became thought of as a **notional** currency whose main use was as the regulating factor in the Exchange Rate Mechanism. More recently there has been steady though not spectacular progress towards the acceptance of the ECU as a commercial currency featuring in everyday inter-community trade and to a lesser but still significant extent in worldwide trade finance. It is quoted spot and forward on foreign exchange markets which also offer pure currency options in ECUs. It can be borrowed or deposited, bonds and notes can be denominated in the currency and it has featured in investment trusts.

Among the trade finance instruments which feature the ECU frequently are letters of credit, bills of exchange and export credit guarantees supporting medium term credit. It is most significantly becoming increasingly recognized as a currency in which commercial quotations for the sale of goods can be expressed, particularly in inter-community deals, with the intention of limiting the risk of exchange movements which would otherwise arise. Usage has been specially prominent where countries whose currencies are not historically strong are involved, and it appears that unless a far greater degree of stability is achieved in the exchange rates of the principal countries engaged in international trade, the ECU is likely to continue to become increasingly attractive to the world trading community.

At the time of writing, an evaluation of the effectiveness of the ERM is taking place within most of the countries who are members, focused on the events leading up to the withdrawal of the pound sterling and the Italian lira from the mechanism in the autumn of 1992. This followed a period during which the economies of Western Europe, in common with many elsewhere in the world, were suffering from prolonged recession but the effects were varied in severity with Germany least affected. Weakness in the exchange rates of currencies other than the deutschmark caused rates of exchange to hover around the point at which intervention was obligatory. To the commercial pressures resulting from a confidence crisis in the currencies based on fears for the future of domestic economies was added in early September 1992 a surge of speculative dealing on foreign exchange markets. The result was massive intervention by central banks throughout member countries, reinforced by equally spectacular rises in interest rates in those members whose currencies were under threat. Despite these actions, which were absolutely correct under the rules of the 'club', rates fell through the lower limits specified for the pound and lira.

The sole alternative remaining was realignment by effectively devaluing these two currencies and revaluing the deutschmark upward. However both Italy and the United Kingdom deemed it more desirable in view of domestic considerations in their countries – as well as in Germany which, sensing a danger of inflation consequent on reunification, was resolutely opposed to lowering its interest rates – to withdraw their currencies from the Exchange Rate Mechanism. Since that time similar pressures have built up against the currencies of other members and have fuelled the debate on the Mechanism. A further crisis had led the remaining members to extend the permitted fluctuation bands.

It is outside our brief to consider the merits of the Mechanism as a means of furthering the aims of the European Monetary System, namely to establish economic and monetary union within the Community: our purpose is merely to look at the effects of the Mechanism on the growth of inter-community trade. In doing so we must however look beyond stability in exchange rates as trade expansion is equally dependent of the control of inflation and the maintenance of a healthy domestic economy; most companies that export do so as a development from a secure domestic trading base.

In an ideal world, international traders would seek immoveable exchange rates (or a world currency); in that in which we have to operate our desire must be that any international efforts are directed to limiting the amount and frequency of changes, thus creating a more stable environment in which trade can both prosper and increase. While each is important if, as seems unavoidable, a choice has to be made between amount and frequency we would probably prefer changes in modest figures at as long an interval as practicable to infrequent but major alterations. The latter were a characteristic of fixed rates of exchange and were usually preceded by an indefinite but significant period during which the commercial world was aware that a change was unavoidable. This had the effect of paralysing trade and was one of the principal reasons for the reversion to floating rates.

The Mechanism in its operations to date has exhibited somewhat conflicting results in influencing rates, and it is probably too early for any general judgement on the system, particularly since recent years have been against a background of exceptionally severe recession. An evaluation of its performance is prudent if not essential if we are to continue to seek improvements to the Mechanism.

The agreement inherent in the parity principle that governments will keep exchange rates under regular review not just for internal purposes but to assess implications must be beneficial to trading interests. So also is the obligation to take action before rates have moved to the limits of the permitted band, as it gives time for corrective measures to take effect and may enable the brake to be applied less violently than would be the case if a disaster point had been reached. Problems arise for individual governments and trading interests when consideration is given to the nature of the corrective measures applied. Intervention in foreign exchange markets, whether or not it succeeds in its aim, has no immediate adverse effects on trading companies and must be a stronger influence on rates if co-ordinated between central banks, as in the Mechanism, than would be the intervention of a single central bank.

It is with the possible side effects of supporting corrective action through changes in interest rates that exporters and importers will take issue. In theory the Mechanism requires that a country whose currency is threatened should increase interest rates which will cause hot money to enter with a consequent rise in demand for the currency, and a country whose currency is towards the upper limit for permitted fluctuations to lower interest rates with a consequent fall in demand. In practice member countries have appeared reluctant to conform to these rules if, by doing so, they were imposing undue strains on their domestic economies.

The United Kingdom for example believed the necessary stimulus to an economy struggling to emerge from recession was attainable only through a lowering of interest rates at a time when the pound's exchange rate against other European currencies required an upward adjustment in interest rates. Similarly Germany has resisted pressure to decrease interest rates, despite the strength of the deutschmark, due to fears of inflationary effects. In the event the volume of selling of sterling and lira was such that even the maintenance of extremely high interest rates over a period could not have avoided a realignment within the Mechanism or the withdrawal which was preferred by the United Kingdom government.

However it is relevant to our consideration of the effect of the Mechanism on international trade to comment that had sterling remained at the expense of prohibitive interest rates this would probably have had the effect of rendering many of our exporters uncompetitive or worse, of jeopardizing their continued existence in both domestic and overseas markets. The debates will continue but those engaging in it are unlikely to have missed the dual lessons that the Mechanism cannot be expected to cure the economic malaise of each of its members and that the volume of business passing through foreign exchange markets is such as to dwarf the intervention of central banks. Our contribution to the discussion can only be that exporters have much to gain if governments continue collectively to address the problems of exchange rate stability with a view to discovering a successful solution.

Avoiding the Spread

If international traders buy and sell currency regularly through the bank, they will of course buy at the bank's selling rate and sell at the bank's buying rate. As we observed, the difference, or spread, between the two rates represents the bank's profit. On a single deal of modest size the spread may seem small; in the table shown in exhibit 4.1 the spread on United States dollar spot rates is 0.1 of a cent, that on the deutschmark spot rate 0.32 of a Pfennig. Where numerous deals take place, however, the cumulative amount represented by spread is considerable and is particularly noticeable if an exporter is both selling finished goods and buying raw materials with invoicing in the same currency. How much better it would prove financially if it could in some way offset purchase costs against sale proceeds. This can indeed be done and is commonplace among established exporters who would not for one moment contribute a greater sum than was necessary to their bank's profits.

As an exporter's business grows, if the inclusion of deals for settlement in currencies other than sterling becomes sufficiently large to ensure that it is cost effective to do so, accounts in the currencies concerned may be considered. They may be opened with banks in the buyers' countries or with the exporter's own bank in the United Kingdom; circumstances will determine the choice. For example, an exporter selling many articles of low value to a variety of buyers in (say) France may find it prohibitive to have the proceeds of each sale remitted to the United Kingdom due to the disproportionate minimum charge on remittance. The answer here would be an account with a French bank to which buyers could make payment and from which periodically remittances of a worthwhile size could be made to the exporter's United Kingdom bank. In this case, although the main benefits would be those resulting from reduced transmission charges (and probably the convenience of buyers), it would also avoid the bank being asked to buy a large number of small amounts in currency, a request which it is unlikely to welcome.

Quite different considerations apply for the company both importing and exporting goods invoiced in the same currency where viable sums for dealing purposes are involved. The main purpose then is to exchange the currency against sterling only when net balances accrue representing profits. It is probably more convenient in this scenario for the account to be opened in currency with the company's United Kingdom bank, which knows the company's management well and is thus able to accept instructions for outward payments with the minimum formality. It will also normally be possible to earn interest on a currency account provided an adequate balance is maintained, although some banks will require an interest free balance below which interest is not paid and others require surplus funds to be placed on deposit to attract interest.

Of course, even when both imports and exports are in the same currency, the time schedule may create problems. An import may have to be settled before the funds resulting from an export are due for payment. In such an event an approach for an agreed overdraft on the currency account can be made in exactly the same manner as for sterling facilities, or in the case

of protracted but easily calculated time intervals many currencies may be borrowed for fixed terms. We must remember, if
considering currency facilities, that the interest rates applying
will be those appropriate to the currency in question irrespective
of the fact that the borrowing may be arranged here in the
United Kingdom, and credit interest if payable to us will be
similarly calculated.

The borrowing of currency may also be used as an alternative
method of eliminating the exchange risk. An exporter selling
goods value DM100,000 could on completion of the contract
with the buyer borrow deutschmarks for a period corresponding with that to settlement and sell immediately in the spot
market for sterling thus protecting profit margins. On receipt of
settlement from the buyer the deutschmarks are immediately
available in repayment of the loan. The appeal of this method
of eliminating risk will depend on an assessment of spot and
forward exchange rates and the rates of interest then current on
both deutschmarks and sterling.

It may be that although interest has to be paid on the
deutschmark borrowing, a higher rate of interest may be obtainable on the sterling produced by the spot sale or, if the
exporter is already in overdraft in sterling, the benefit in
reduced interest may be conclusive in the choice of whether
to borrow and sell the currency immediately. One should
perhaps also add that obviously the liability contracted as a
result of a currency loan is as real as that involved when the
exporter borrows sterling, and the exporter must therefore
ensure that prior agreement is received from its bank for any
facility contemplated.

Euro-Currency Markets

The ability of banks to offer a service to their customers whereby
they can deposit or advance foreign currency must depend on
the existence of a market in which the banks themselves can
borrow or lend the currencies concerned. This is known as the
Euro-Currency Market. The term Euro-Currency itself calls for
some explanation: what is a Euro-Currency, and how does it

differ from any other currency? A currency is always held in accounts domiciled in the country concerned; deutschmarks, for example, are always held in an account in Germany. The ownership of those deutschmarks will however be divided between residents of Germany and non-residents. British banks who are maintaining accounts denominated in deutschmarks for exporters (or importers) do not hold the deutschmarks concerned, as they would sterling, but deposit them in turn with a German bank as part of the working balance in that currency which the United Kingdom bank may require at any one time. Those deutschmarks and any others which are owned by non-residents of Germany are known as **Euro-Marks**. Similarly, United States dollars owned by non-residents of the United States are termed **Euro-Dollars**, French francs owned by non-residents of France as **Euro-Francs** and so on for other currencies. The generic term for all such currencies is **Euro-Currency**.

Exhibit 4.6: London Foreign Exchange Market – Eurocurrencies Interest Rates

	7 days	X July 19XX 1 Month	3 Months	6 Months
Dollars	3-3.0625	3-3.0625	3.125- 3.1875	3.3125- 3.34375
Marks	7-7.25	7.125-7.25	7-7.125	6.8125- 6.9375
Swiss Francs	4.6875- 4.8125	4.5625- 4.6875	4.5625- 4.6875	4.4375- 4.5625
Yen	3.1875- 3.3125	3.125-3.25	3.0625- 3.1875	3-3.125

Notes: The above rates are those quoted daily in the Press but many other currencies can be quoted upon request.

For comparison purposes the Finance Houses Base Rate for Sterling on the day in question was 6%.

It is beyond our brief to trace the history of the Euro-Currency Market but its inception with Euro-Dollars owed much to the fact that they were free from the domestic regulations of the Federal Reserve and, in general, the concept depends on the flexibility and reliability which freedom from domestic controls bestows on Euro-Currencies.

Unlike other currencies those dealt with on the Euro-Market are not bought and sold but are lent or borrowed. The rates are published daily and to complete our examples of how currency rates are quoted exhibit 4.6 shows the manner in which Euro-Currency interest rates might appear. The United Kingdom has become the major centre for Euro-Currency dealing, with the important exception of Euro-Sterling (sterling which is held by non-residents of the United Kingdom) which has its principle market in Paris.

Tender to Contract Cover

To complete our overview of foreign exchange we shall return, as promised in chapter 2, to the possibility of eliminating or reducing the exchange risk in relation to large projects for which exporters tender in foreign currency, using credit insurance. As noted earlier a foreign exchange forward contract is a firm commitment to deliver currency or sterling at a fixed future date or between two such dates. A tenderer has no means of discovering if the tender will be successful or not until the adjudication takes place and contracts are awarded. If it is required to tender in foreign currency the exporting company must calculate the amount based on a rate of exchange which is known at the time of tender (assume the spot rate). If that rate alters before any contract is awarded it may well find that its projected profit has disappeared.

Similarly, you will comment, for the exporter quoting a potential buyer who may or may not choose to accept the quote. This is correct, but the risk is much greater, firstly because tenders are usually for large value contracts, and secondly the period from tender to adjudication, typically three months or more, is much longer than that between a quotation and its acceptance or rejection. Unfortunately for the tenderer, if it elects to endeavour to eliminate this risk by covering forward, an equally dangerous possibility arises: that of the tender being rejected with the consequent inability to deliver currency under the contract.

The Export Credits Guarantee Department (ECGD) offers to exporters in this position a scheme whereby they may declare the tender transaction and the department will provide a list of forward exchange rates based on the estimated payment date if the contract is secured. The exporter is guaranteed payment of a sterling sum based on these rates. If the tender is successful the exporter is expected immediately to enter into a foreign exchange forward contract. Upon payment and delivery of the currency to the bank the exporter must declare to the department the sterling sum realized. If this falls short of the guaranteed sum the Export Credits Guarantee Department pays the shortfall, to the extent that it exceeds 1 per cent of the sum guaranteed, up to a maximum of 25 per cent of that value. Should the sum received under the foreign exchange forward contract exceed that guaranteed the excess is payable to the department. Thus the tenderer may submit the tender in the knowledge that exchange risk is substantially reduced.

5

Agreeing a Method of Payment

There is no better guide to export payment practice than the lessons learnt in the hard school of experience and at this stage in our review let us pause and examine the main causes for losses suffered in the past by companies involved in international trade. They may conveniently be grouped under three headings.

Risks Associated with the Country or the Buyer

These will include those dealt with in chapter 2 and may be summarized as the economic and political dangers in the country and the dishonesty, inefficiency or bankruptcy of the buyer. The necessary homework to minimize the risks has been adequately covered with the important exception of the buyer's inefficiency. True this may be a contributory factor in any adverse trade or financial report but it is well to remember that, unlike dishonesty or bankruptcy, it can be to a significant degree corrected by the exporter setting out in abundantly clear terms the basis for payment (the method to be adopted and the means of settlement within that method). For example there are a number of ways by which payment can be made under the general method of 'open account'. These important clarifications in regard to method and settlement will be emphasized in this and later chapters as each individual method of payment is explained.

Movements in rates of exchange

The nature of the exchange risk and the means whereby it can be minimized formed the subject of chapter 4 but it will be necessary, where appropriate, to comment on any references which should be made to the fact that invoicing is in currency when arranging the method of payment. Such comments will again be included in the explanation of the method and the actions called for by the exporter to ensure it operates smoothly.

Administrative and procedural misunderstandings

This category unfortunately ranks high on the list of reasons for loss, and includes a wide variety of omissions and errors. The granting of credit is a prime example. We have seen, in reviewing credit to the buyer, the importance of researching the buyer to determine if the length and amount of credit extended are justified but loss does occur due to the exporter failing to appreciate that both are involved as separate issues. I have known otherwise experienced exporters who have failed completely to understand the principles underlying the granting of discounts. If an exporter agrees to a discount if payment is made within 60 days it must be clearly understood that 'cleared funds' are required within the 60 days. On many occasions the discount is unthinkingly given when all that has happened within the time limit is that a piece of paper which may or may not produce the desired payment has been received by the exporter. The adverse effects of such slack control or misunderstanding of procedures, will be seen when we consider the 'open account' method of payment later in this chapter.

A failure accurately to cost exports, transportation and insurance charges for example is an administrative mistake which will destroy the build up of a quotation described in chapter 3, as will any underestimate or omission of component or raw material costs. The dangers of loss arising from agreement to an inappropriate method of payment or failure correctly to assess the cost of the chosen method are real and now that we are beginning our examination of the methods available it is vital that there is understanding of what can and cannot be achieved through each. As a workman assesses the task he is asked to undertake, the tools available and which is the correct one to select to ensure a first class result, so we as exporters must display the same professional approach. Finance methods are also varied and choice should reflect individual circumstances.

The last but by no means least of the causes for loss lies in a lack of communication. This can be between exporter and buyer as in the case of a failure to agree on the exact documentation required in support of a shipment, or between the exporter and the intermediary, say a bank. A method of payment is only capable of yielding the required result if the principles and procedures inherent are both understood and followed. In our examination of methods, we will endeavour therefore to identify both to avoid the perceived pitfalls.

The Role of the Credit Controller

Exporting is above all a team effort and the executives of a company hoping to succeed in overseas markets all have their individual parts to play. In the payment area one key role is that of credit control. Depending on the size of the company this may be carried out by the managing director, finance director, chief accountant or credit controller; for convenience we will assume the last named is responsible. As an examiner for the Institute of Export I posed a question several years ago to candidates sitting for the professional qualification: 'describe the role of a credit controller'. Surprisingly a large percentage of answers pictured the controller as having a predominantly passive contribution which could be summarized as monitoring outstanding invoices and, as the interval by which payment was overdue grew, making increasingly strong demands for settlement culminating perhaps in enlisting specialized help in collecting the debt.

Without underestimating the importance of monitoring, particularly if the assistance of modern computer techniques is used to the full, the company which uses its credit controller solely in this passive way is lacking in foresight unless some other executive is taking the necessary action to prove 'prevention is better than cure'. The controller should be involved in the initial discussions as to whether a potential new market is worthy of development; while his colleagues will comment on such questions as commercial demand, marketing problems, and transportation considerations it is his place to pronounce on financial viability of 'country risk'.

It is often the dispassionate view of the controller which tempers the commission oriented enthusiasm of the sales representative for new contracts. Likewise the assessment of exchange risk and the costing underlying the choice of delivery terms demand his involvement in conjunction with his counterparts in the shipping and production areas. The determination of the extent and duration of any credit offered require his recommendation as does the agreement of the method of payment to be adopted. It is the controller's skill in establishing a rapport with colleagues which ensures that when the inevitable crisis arises – a withdrawal of labour, a breakdown in machinery or delay in dispatch – he or she is immediately advised and able to take all possible steps to avoid a major financial disaster occurring. Only at the conclusion of all these essentially active roles does the dual responsibility of efficient monitoring and 'chasing' begin. A final attribute of this key contributor to a trouble free payment is the ability of controllers to be selective in their approach to outstanding debts; a hasty, heavy handed demand to a long standing customer a short time overdue for the first time can be as destructive as a lack of firmness in dealing with the persistent offender which will brand the company as an 'easy touch'.

The principles involved in the choice

When applying the results of their research to a recommendation on the desirable method of payment, controllers will follow the practice in this book of recognizing the practicalities of exporting as well as the theory. Thus the harsh realities of competition will again be to the fore and may mean that concessions to the buyer's views on payment method are unavoidable. Despite these constraints it is important to remember throughout the negotiations the three main considerations determining the acceptability of the method finally agreed: the security implicit or obtainable by observing the correct procedure, the speed of settlement which involves both the method chosen and the means by which remittance is sought under that method and the costs incurred.

It is necessary in consequence to look at these considerations separately when examining each method although, to avoid the problems of updating and variations between banks in charging, it will be necessary to confine ourselves to relative costs of the methods. Fortunately with the current emphasis on openness in regard to charges, which in the opinion of the author is as helpful to exporters as to any other group using banks, the costs of most services available to companies trading internationally are included in published tariffs. Examination candidates and other practising exporters are urged to seek copies of one of these tariffs if they are not already held.

Types of Methods of Payment

Provided we have a choice of method and we have observed that in some instances the use of a particular method is obligatory under the regulations of the importing country or is mandatory if we wish to obtain credit insurance, that choice lies between the following: payment in advance, open account, bills for collection or documents against payment and documentary letters of credit.

We must not confuse methods of finance, which will be examined in a later chapter, with those for payment. Using an outside provider of finance may affect the procedure adopted, for example the condition for the finance may be that shipping documents are routed through the provider, but the contractual provisions for payment will still require one of the above methods of payment to be agreed. Now let us look at each of the methods in turn.

Payment in advance or cash with order

Without doubt payment in advance meets all the exporter's requirements: it poses no security problem, provided the correct settlement means are employed it is speedy and the costs are identical with those of using open account, namely less than those for either bills or letters of credit. Conversely it is a very risky method when viewed by the importer who has no safeguard against non-delivery of the goods except the rights of redress contained in the contract for the sale; the exporter holds both payment and goods until such time as shipment is made. For this reason payment in advance is normally relatively rare and confined to the following circumstances:

1 Where the buyer's domicile represents such a high country risk that the exporter is only prepared to do business on these terms.

2 Where a seller's market exists – that is where the buyer is unlikely to be able to purchase goods of the same type of quality at a comparable price from an alternative supplier – in these circumstances the seller is clearly able to dictate payment terms and while perhaps not insisting on payment in advance if the prospects of continuing profitable business are good, it is probable that a one-off order will elicit a request for that method.

3 Where an order involves goods which must be specially manufactured and are not available off the shelf. This will mean that the exporter runs a serious risk that should the order be cancelled after manufacture or the buyer default on payment the goods may not be saleable elsewhere or any sale will only be made after considerable delay or at a lower price than envisaged. It is usual for recognition of the risk to be through an agreement for all or at least part of the payment to be made in advance, depending on the size of the order and degree of specialization.

For large projects, usually involving capital goods, where the costs of financing manufacturing would be so high as to be impossible for even a major firm or multinational to meet if no payment were to be forthcoming until completion of the project, it is usual for a number of advance payments to be made at various stages in the performance of the contract, often against bankers' guarantees which are described in a later chapter.

Open account trading

This method is widely used in exporting particularly where business has been conducted between the parties over a considerable period. It is also used for a very high percentage of trading between members of the European Community (recently estimated at over 70 per cent) and as the proportion of such exports to the total of the United Kingdom's exports is consistently rising it is imperative our exporters have a sound understanding of this method. With the current emphasis in the media and in Department of Trade and Industry publications on treating Europe as an extension of the domestic market, it seems likely that open account settlement will become even more significant in inter-community trade.

It is fortunate that we are considering this method so soon after probing and stressing the role of the credit controller. Open account offers minimal security to the exporter and maximum advantage to the buyer. The goods are dispatched direct to the buyer and he is sent the necessary documentation to arrange clearance. Dependent upon the terms agreed between the parties payment will be due either on receipt of the goods or after the expiration of the period of credit stipulated in the contract. In either event the buyer is in the position of having the goods in his possession before having to make payment while the exporter has dispatched documents of title to the goods and is left entirely relying on the buyer's honesty and integrity. If these attributes are missing it is small consolation to the exporter that he may have the legal right to proceed against the buyer in the event of default. With this method of payment the value of the credit controller's diligence in making the necessary enquiries to minimize buyer and country risk (see chapter 2) is evident.

Because of the lack of inherent security, open account is ideally used only in certain circumstances.

1 Exporters, from a reasonable length of experience in dealing with the buyer or from the replies received to trade and financial enquiries, are confident that payment will be made in full on or before the agreed payment date.

2 The same confidence is present after enquiries have revealed that the buyer is regarded as 'undoubted' and is probably therefore an internationally known name which would consider any suggestion of dealing on other than open account terms as mildly insulting to its standing.

In respect of this category it is important to stress that in times of severe recession there is a danger that firms previously thought undoubted may be threatened and it is necessary to be doubly sure before accepting this standing unless the financial report using the terms is current; it is also emphasized that a buyer may purport to be undoubted as a means of inducing the exporter to agree to open account; it is the repetition of that description by a reputable bank or credit agency which is conclusive.

3 When an exporting company is selling to a parent, subsidiary or associated company overseas.

4 If the competition faced is such that exporters are forced into matching in price and method of payment the terms offered by others even if, in normal circumstances, they would have stood out for a securer method of payment.

In this instance it is relevant to make two comments: if the enquiries made on the buyer suggest that the exporter's preference for an alternative method should be absolute and not marginal it would probably be wiser to forego the business: and if credit insurance is obtainable it will enable the exporter to accept, albeit reluctantly, the less secure open account method.

If there is a limited amount of action which can be taken to improve the security under this method of payment much more can be attempted in the endeavour to improve the speed of settlement. Of course some buyers will take advantage of the 'informal' nature of the method, with the absence of any intermediaries through whom shipping documents are to pass, to delay payment in an effort to improve cash flow. It will be argued that only buyer and seller are aware of any delay unlike some other methods which draw the attention of banks to any tardiness with possible serious effects on the credit reputation of the buyer.

In fact, as we are increasingly aware in the United Kingdom and elsewhere, deliberate slow paying is a disease which is highly contagious and adds significantly to the economic and social damage caused in recessionary times. So much so that it seems probable some legislative sanctions will be attempted within the foreseeable future. However many buyers do not deliberately delay payment but instinctively turn to the methods of remittance best known to them in domestic trade unaware that these may be inefficient in international settlements. In considering the various methods of remittance available it is important to influence the buyer's choice to our company's advantage. Among the reasons for loss listed earlier in this chapter was the inefficient buyer; perhaps if we can communicate our requests on settlement in a simple, clear fashion we can minimize the adverse effects from that cause.

Methods of Remittance

There is no obligatory method of remittance. Payment upon receipt of the goods or at the end of any credit period extended may be made by any type of remittance agreed between the exporter and buyer. Perhaps in using the word 'agreed' one is making an illogical assumption. I often suspect that in a high proportion of deals no mention is made in correspondence between the parties about how remittance should be handled. This omission will probably cause little distress to the buyer, although the inexperienced might appreciate a suggestion, but can be expensive to the exporter. As with other negotiable matters the exporter cannot demand a particular method of remittance but will be well advised to request one. The choices available to a buyer for remitting payments due under open account trading are as follows.

SWIFT transfers

This is a relatively recent addition to the inter-bank transfer system, SWIFT; the letters stand for the Society for Worldwide Inter-bank Financial Telecommunication. The initial subscriber banks numbered over 400 and were spread throughout the major trading nations. Since that time the system has grown substantially and is rapidly replacing the previous cable, telegraphic and mail transfers which will however continue to be used by non-members of SWIFT. Benefits to the international trading community are that instructions for transfers once approved can be transmitted in minutes, those to the banks include the ability of the system to incorporate authentication procedures. The terminology used divides instructions into those for express international money transfers (broadly identical with the previous cable or telegraphic transfer) and those for international money transfer (the successor to the previous mail transfer). You will often find the divisions abbreviated to EIMT and IMT respectively, and the descriptions priority and non-priority are also in use.

It is often helpful to exporters in requesting buyers to remit through the inter-bank system to be aware of the instructions which the buyer's bank will require. Forms in use may vary slightly from country to country or from bank to bank but such variations will be minor. Exhibit 5.1 shows a specimen of the forms used by one of the United Kingdom clearing banks and these are worth study as a guide to the information an exporter should convey to its buyer if an international money transfer is required in payment. Special attention is drawn to the following.

The form provides for the currency to be remitted to be specified. Remember in chapter 4 it was noted that the currency invoiced was that in which payment was due; here is the implementation of that understanding.

The remitting bank will make payment through a bank in the exporter's country which will either send the amount to him, pay him on application, or credit any account he holds with them dependent on the buyer's instructions through his bank. The quickest of these three options is a credit to the exporter's account as it will avoid clearance time on a cheque which will

Exhibit 5.1: Express International Money Transfer

Lloyds Bank	**Application for Express International Money Transfer**	For International Money Transfer (Not Express) use Form 55D 55C

To Lloyds Bank Plc   Please complete by Typewriter or in Block Capitals in Ball Point Pen
Please make the following Transfer: Date_____

Branch Title and Sorting Code Number		Please Debit my/our* Sterling*/ _____ † Currency* Account
		Sterling Account Number Currency Account Number
		0 □□□□□□□ □□□□□□□

Remitter's Name	

			Amount	Currency
Amount of Payment (see note 2 overleaf)	□	Remit in Foreign Currency the sum of		
(Tick appropriate box)	□	Remit the Foreign Currency equivalent of Sterling	£	
	□	Remit in Sterling the sum of	£	

Amount in words	

Beneficiary · Quote Full Name · Quote Address unless to be paid to a Bank A/c	
Beneficiary's Account Number (if any)	
Details of Payment Information for the Beneficiary (see note 3 overleaf)	
Beneficiary's Bank (if applicable) (see note 4 overleaf)	

Method of Payment	Payment will be made direct to Beneficiary/Beneficiary's account unless indicated below
Tick if appropriate	□ Pay to Beneficiary on Application and Identification

Charges (see note 6 overleaf)	Lloyds Bank charges to be paid by the remitter and the foreign bank's charges by the beneficiary. If otherwise, indicate below by placing a tick in the appropriate box:
	□ All charges to be paid by remitter Charges to be debited to (if different from above)
	□ All charges to be paid by beneficiary Account Number □□□□□□

Foreign Exchange Details (if appropriate) (Remember Lloyds Bank sells the Currency)	Rate	Date Booked/Agreed*	If to be applied against a Forward Contract also quote:
	F. E. Ref.	Value Date	Contract No. _____
	Correspondent Bank	Position Ref.	Maturity/ Option Date(s) _____

FOR BANK USE ONLY	F. E. Code B*/F*/X*	Cross Rate	Market Segment Code □□□

Special Instructions CBD*/LBCS* Hold entries? Y*/N*	Lloyds Bank Charges Currency □□□ Amount	

Authorised Signatory (ies) Confirmed for Lloyds Bank Plc (GRB. INL. 4.1)	Confirmed with customer (if appropriate)	Date	IMT/Branch Ref. Number	Funds Transfer Number

Input By:	Authorised By:	Released By:

Lloyds Bank Plc is registered in England no 2065
Registered office: 71 Lombard Street, London EC3P 3BS
Member of IMRO, and the Banking Ombudsman Scheme.
A Signatory to the Code of Banking Practice.
*delete as appropriate
†insert name of currency

Customer copy

Important: Please see note 1 overleaf for Banks Conditions for Effecting the Transfer. (Part 2 to be originally signed)	Address _____
Signature _____	_____

otherwise be issued. It is therefore in the exporter's interest to advise the buyer of the bank, branch and account number to which payment is to be directed. Frequently experienced exporters arrange for these particulars to be printed on their invoice heads.

To avoid disruption to remittance due to misunderstandings about who is to pay charges the form provides for the remitting bank's charges to be paid by the buyer and those of the bank in the exporter's country to be met by the exporter **unless** it has previously been agreed that one party will pay all charges, in which case space is allowed for this agreement to be reflected in the instruction. The exporter should therefore ensure that his request to the buyer should reiterate any agreement on charges previously reached.

Although of no significance to the exporter it is interesting to note that the form provides for the buyer to insert details of any foreign exchange forward contract entered into for payment thus ensuring this is not overlooked; if a spot deal is effected it would have to be reversed.

The form shown in exhibit 5.1 covers an **express** international money transfer. This will be more expensive in charges than the international money transfer, but in deciding which to request the buyer to use and how charges are to be divided the exporter will need to consider the amount being remitted and interest rates prevailing at the time of transfer.

Telegraphic and mail transfer

Still an effective means of making settlement through the inter-bank system when one or more of the banks to be used are not members of SWIFT and the computerized benefits are not therefore available. The procedures are basically the same as those described under 'SWIFT transfers'.

Banker's draft

The buyer may choose to request its bank to issue a draft on its banking correspondent in the exporter's country and to debit the amount to the buyer's account together with the bank's charges for issue. The draft is then dispatched by the buyer to the exporter who arranges collection. To the extent that the draft is drawn by one bank on another it represents a more acceptable document to the exporter than would the buyer's own cheque but the method suffers from the risk of loss in transit. This is particularly troublesome as a banker's draft bears the normal undertaking to pay inherent in its own paper (cheques, notes or bills of exchange for which it is the payer) and issuing banks are in consequence extremely reluctant to dishonour even if the payee bank has made payment to other than the rightful holder. In order to issue a new draft in place of one reported lost the issuing bank will normally request an indemnity from its customer; a practice which is rightly regarded as a real liability by the indemnifier and is an inconvenience to the buyer.

The costs of issuing a draft are normally similar to those for an international money transfer but it will be apparent from the above description that an exporter will prefer the latter. An example of an application for a banker's draft appears in exhibit 5.2.

International Money Orders (IMOs)

Some banks will sell to buyers an international money order which they can forward to the exporter in a similar manner to the banker's draft. The difference is that an international money order is sold off the shelf and the number of currencies in which they are issued (and on occasion the amounts) may be limited. The principle is not unlike postal orders and the charges for issue are lower than those for banker's draft as they are preprinted and therefore consume less time to issue. The position in the event of loss in transit is identical to that of banker's drafts.

Exhibit 5.2: Application for Foreign Draft

Lloyds Bank

Application for Foreign Draft   55H

To Lloyds Bank Plc   Please complete by Typewriter or in Block Capitals in Ball Point Pen
Please supply a Draft as below: Date_____

Branch Title and Sorting Code Number		Please Debit my/our* Sterling*/ _____ † Currency* Account	
		Sterling Account Number	Currency Account Number
		0 ☐☐☐☐☐☐	☐☐☐☐☐☐

			Amount	Currency
Amount of Draft (see notes overleaf)	☐	In Foreign Currency the sum of		
(Tick appropriate box)	☐	In the Foreign Currency equivalent of Sterling	£	
	☐	In Sterling the sum of	£	

Amount in words

Payable to

Lloyds Bank Charges (Tick appropriate box)	☐ To be deducted from amount of Draft	Charges to be debited to (if different from above)
	☐ To be added to cost of Draft	Account Number ☐☐☐☐☐☐

For Sterling Drafts only Country Draft to be drawn on (see note overleaf)

Foreign Exchange Details (if appropriate)	Rate	Date Booked/Agreed*	If to be applied against a Forward Contract also quote:
(Remember Lloyds Bank sells the Currency)	F. E./Positioning Ref.		Contract No. _____
	Correspondent Bank		Maturity/ Option Date(s) _____

FOR BANK USE ONLY (GRB. INL. 4.1 Refers) Confirmed for Lloyds Bank Plc	Cross Rate	F. E. Code B* / F* / X*
Authorised Signatory (ies) _____	Lloyds Bank Charges Currency ☐☐☐ Amount_____	
	Date	Market Segment Code ☐☐☐
	IMT/Branch Ref No.	Funds Transfer No.

Input by	Authorised by	Released by

I/we understand that should this draft, through no fault of Lloyds Bank Plc, be unpaid, I/we can only reclaim the sterling value thereof at the buying rate of the day when the refund takes place. The refund cannot be effected until I/we return the draft and Lloyds Bank Plc have received definite advice from their Correspondent that the draft is unpaid, and that the original instructions have been cancelled. Where local exchange control regulations exist in the beneficiary's country there may be an additional delay in the return of the funds.

(Part 2 to be originally signed)

Name _____

Address _____   ☐ Please hold Draft for collection

_____   ☐ Please post Draft to my/our address
(Tick appropriate box)

Customer Copy

Signature _____

Buyer's cheque

Of all methods of remittance available for settlement of open account transactions the use of a buyer's cheque on its local bank is the least satisfactory to the exporter. It not only carries the risk of dishonour on presentation, as compared with a banker's draft or international money order which are both drawn on a bank, but can often be the slowest of the remittance methods.

Imagine **PDB Exports (93) Ltd** have sold on 90-day credit terms to **XSUD Imports Inc.** of Wyoming Creek USA payment to be on open account and that the buyers, in the absence of any agreement about how remittance is to be made, have elected to draw their cheque in settlement on the **First National Farmers Bank Wyoming Creek**. Taking by way of illustration the worst possible scenario, what is the likely time schedule? 88 days from the receipt of goods XSUD draw their cheque which is mailed to **PDB Exports** who will receive it after the 90 days credit have elapsed but, more importantly, it does not represent cleared funds.

To achieve the position of having such funds PDB Exports will hand the cheque to their British bank for collection which incidentally will be effected at their expense unless any prior arrangements have been concluded with XSUD that the latter will meet collection charges. As there are a large number of banks in the United States of which only a small number have account relationships with banks overseas and many local banks have few branches (sometimes one only), it is unlikely that the British bank receiving the cheque will have a relationship with the First National Farmers Bank Wyoming Creek. The cheque will therefore be mailed to the British bank's correspondent bank (the bank with which it has both authentication and account facilities), nearest to Wyoming Creek with the request that they arrange presentation.

Upon receipt the correspondent bank will act on the British bank's instruction forwarding the cheque to the buyer's bank and provided funds are available the buyer's bank will honour the presentation. Payment will be sent by that bank to the British bank's correspondent which will credit their principal's account, mailing an advice that this has been done. The exporter may be able to request its bank to ask for advice of payment to be cabled at extra cost.

It is apparent that the procedure for collecting will involve considerable time and in effect the exporter will have involuntarily extended much more than the agreed 90 days credit before receiving cleared funds in its account. If the buyer has chosen to adopt the cheque method of payment because the extra credit is needed, as distinct from that being the normal means of settling domestic debts, it would have been preferable for extended terms to have been negotiated at an appropriate price. Lest it be thought from the example given that exporters should never willingly accept the buyer's cheque as a settlement method, it may well be acceptable between parties who have dealt with each other for a considerable time, particularly if the agreed price contains a reasonable profit margin. In other circumstances where new or less well-known buyers are involved an exporter should make every endeavour to receive payment through an alternative means.

6

Documentary Collections

In chapter 5 we have seen that if exporters consider the status report they obtain through their bank on the buyer to be sufficiently strong, they may agree open account as a method of payment, and that this method may also be acceptable where the status report is not quite so strong but credit insurance has been arranged. Earlier in chapter 2 it was also noted that some status reports are extremely guarded, recommending that dealings be conducted only on a secured basis, and that in such circumstances the exporter should think in terms of a letter of credit, which we shall see in later chapters to be a method of payment which can be excellent security.

What happens, however, in the very common situation for exporters where, unless competition makes it essential and the risk is not totally unacceptable, they are reluctant to agree open account terms but equally appreciate that a request for a documentary credit, with the consequent liability considerations and costs for the buyer, is unlikely to be acceptable? In addition, it is often in exporters' minds that the results of their trade and financial enquiries have presented a marginal choice; they would like security initially but the potential buyer appears likely to warrant open account trading after a relatively short period of trading on more secure terms. It is in these circumstances that the method of payment known as bills for collections (documentary collections) or documents against payment is particularly useful.

113

A point worth remembering and not always recognized in examinations of this method is that in addition to the security it provides to the exporters, not as great as a letter of credit but much improved on the minimal protection under open account, it gives similar security to the buyer. Why, you may ask, should the buyers require security, what risk do they run? The answer is that many buyers harbour doubts about unknown sellers: will they ship satisfactorily, will the goods be of the required standard, will the documents covering the shipment be as agreed and appropriate to the delivery term quoted? Much of this anxiety can be avoided by this method of payment, provided the parties concerned understand the procedures required.

Once again we are reminded that any lack of understanding is a potential reason for loss. The documentary collection, as its name implies, confers security on the parties through control of the shipping documents (including any document of title to the goods) which are dealt with through the banking system whether with or without a bill of exchange. Before exploring the procedures we must be aware of the nature of a bill of exchange since if it is not properly drawn up we may find the effectiveness of those procedures seriously impaired.

The Bill of Exchange

While it is not, in general, the purpose here to examine the legal framework for exporting – this is the subject of a companion book in this series – it is necessary as an exception to look at the legal definition of a bill of exchange, since without it we shall be unaware if a vital document included in the collection may be relied upon to perform its function. The definition is as follows:

A bill of exchange is an unconditional order in writing, addressed by one person to another, signed by the person giving it, requiring the person to whom it is addressed to pay on demand, or at a fixed or determinable future time, a sum certain in money to, or to the order of, a specified person (or to bearer).

The parentheses around the last three words are my addition and do not appear in the legal definition. The reason is a practical one; although in other contexts bills of exchange may be drawn payable to bearer it would be extremely rare for this to occur in relation to the settlement of international trade, and it was felt that the unbracketed form might be unintentionally misleading.

As some of the phrases in the definition need explanation, which is easier if we are able to see examples, exhibits 6.1 and 6.2 illustrate a typical sight and usance bill of exchange; usance indicating that the bill is payable a specified number of days after sight. The number of days will normally correspond with the credit period extended by the exporter to the buyer.

Exhibit 6.1: Specimen of Sight Bill of Exchange

No 6842   for £5,000   Date 28th February 1994

At sight pay this sole Bill of Exchange to the order of PDB Exports (93) Ltd the sum of Five Thousand pounds value received

To Alltypes Import Ltd   For and on behalf of
Anytown   PDB Exports (93) Ltd
Anywhere Overseas   22 Arcade Square
       UK Town
       N J Blissom
       Director

There are three parties to a bill of exchange.

1 **The Drawer** who is the exporter issuing (or drawing) the bill; in our examples PDB Exports (93) Ltd.
2 **The Drawee**, the party on whom the bill is drawn and, in the context of international trade, the importer. In exhibit 6.1

this is Alltypes Import Ltd and in exhibit 6.2 Anysort Imports Ltd.

3 **The Payee**, the person to whom the amount of the bill is to be paid. Since it is usual but not invariable in an export transaction for the drawer and payee to be the same, PDB Exports (93) Ltd appears in both examples as the payee. Where the parties are identical it is quite common for the word 'ourselves' to be inserted as payee.

Consider the examples in conjunction with the definition of a bill of exchange and note the precautions taken in order to ensure the documents are properly drawn.

Exhibit 6.2: Specimen of Usance Bill of Exchange

No 2486   Exchange for US $10,000   15th April 1994

At 90 days after sight pay this first of exchange second of the same date and tenor being unpaid to the order of PDB Exports (93) Ltd Ten Thousand United States dollars value received

To Anysort Imports Ltd   For and on behalf of
Any Street   PDB Exports (93) Ltd
Anyplace Overseas   22 Arcade Square
                                          UK Town
                                          N J Blissom
                                          Director

An unconditional order

The examples are unequivocal as regards payment. 'Pay' in the body of a bill is an order not even with a term of politeness such as 'please' or 'kindly' which would be inappropriate in this context. A bill would be improperly drawn if a condition was introduced for example 'pay provided goods delivered in accordance with pro-forma invoice' or 'pay dependent upon carriage per SS Goodfellow Mac'. While such additions might reflect a genuine concern on the part of the buyer, the contract for the sale of the goods is the correct document in which to include stipulations, not the bill of exchange. A statement of fact such as that in exhibit 6.2 'second of the same date and tenor being unpaid' is however valid and refers to a second (or duplicate) bill in the set. The drawing of bills in a set of two is quite usual and is designed to restrict the difficulties arising if the bank splits shipping documents into two remittances, one of which is lost in transit.

Addressed by one person to another

The persons referred to are, of course, the drawer in our examples PDB Exports (93) Ltd and the drawee, Alltypes Import Ltd in exhibit 6.1 and Anysort Imports Ltd in exhibit 6.2.

Signed by the person giving it

The bill must be signed by the drawer. In our examples it is assumed that N.J. Blissom, as a director of PDB Exports (93) Ltd, is an official mandated to sign bills of exchange for and on behalf of the company.

. . . to pay on demand or at a fixed or determinable future time

A bill is payable on demand if it requires under its terms payment 'on demand', 'at sight' or 'on presentation'. Thus the bill shown in exhibit 6.1 is a sight bill. The interpretation of a fixed or determinable future time requires some clarification. A bill payable 90 days after sight, as in exhibit 6.2, is clearly a fixed or determinable time, as would be 90 days after date, and these are usance (time allowed) bills. An insertion, 'payable on the arrival of the vessel Goodfellow Mac' would however render the bill invalid; the vessel's date of arrival is not only unknown, except as an estimate, it is not certain – the vessel may sink during the journey. Similarly the phrase 'on or before', which is common usage in so many other business contexts, is unacceptable when applied to payment of a bill of exchange; it is a variable date and not therefore determinable as required by the definition.

A sum certain in money

The definition precludes by the use of the word 'certain' any variations for example 'about', 'up to', or 'not exceeding'. The amount must be exact but, as evidenced in our examples, it can be in any currency, the bill in exhibit 6.1 being expressed in sterling, while that in exhibit 6.2 is drawn in US Dollars. Naturally it would not be acceptable to include an alternative; payable for '£10,000 or US$16,000', but clausing designed to determine the rate of exchange applied in settlement or interest payable is permissible and will be described later in this chapter.

The life cycle of a bill of exchange

An exporter will sell goods to the buyer either for immediate payment, in which case a sight bill will be drawn, or for payment at the conclusion of an agreed period of credit, say 90 days, in which case a bill payable 90 days after sight will be issued. The term 'sight' means exactly that, the day upon which the bill is sighted by the drawee (buyer).

Bills may be 'clean', that is, they have no supporting documentation or 'documentary', which means they are supported by the documentation covering the shipment of the goods. Clean bills are normally used in international trade where the export is not of goods but of a service, and there is in consequence no shipment, or where the shipping documents have, for a variety of reasons, been sent separately to the buyer. Perhaps, for example, an exporter who has dealt on what are virtually open account terms, might decide to seek an overdue payment by using a sight bill referring to the outstanding invoice, thus enabling presentation through a bank whose mere intervention might facilitate payment.

When a bill is presented to the drawee, if it is payable on sight, the presentation will itself trigger the settlement process unless the bill is dishonoured. A usance bill, in contrast, is accepted by the drawee but it is not payable until the maturity date. Acceptance is accomplished by the drawee writing 'accepted payable on the . . .' on the face of the bill and signing. The date shown for payment, which is also known as the maturity date, is calculated in accordance with the usance of the bill; a bill drawn payable 90 days after sight, for example, would have inserted in the acceptance the date 90 days after that upon which the drawee first sighted the bill.

A usance bill which has been accepted by the drawee becomes a most valuable document in the payment for the export. In accepting, the drawee (buyer), who by that act becomes the acceptor, assumes responsibility for paying on the maturity date and that responsibility exists irrespective of the contract for the sale of goods; an important simplification in the event of the exporter having to resort to legal action. After acceptance the bill may be returned to the exporter for retention until maturity or, if presentation is through a bank, the accepted bill may be held for presenting on maturity for payment. If it is returned to the exporter he may choose to endeavour to discount the bill for immediate cash with a third party, such as his bank. When this occurs the third party pays the amount of the bill less the discount charge to the exporter and becomes a holder in due course of the bill. He will present the bill on maturity to the acceptor for payment and acquires on discounting all rights against the acceptor which the exporter enjoyed.

Normally the discount (or negotiation) of the bills is 'with recourse' to the drawer although in certain instances it may be 'without recourse', in which case the discount charge will be higher. 'With recourse' signifies that, should the bill be dishonoured by the acceptor on being presented for payment, the holder has the right to demand payment from the drawer. Although it is unusual in normal international trade for a bill of exchange to be discounted more than once, it is quite legal for this to happen. When it does the ultimate holder who presents for payment at maturity has the right to recourse not only to the drawer but to all subsequent holders (who will have endorsed the bill) in the event of dishonour. More will be said about the bill of exchange as a method of finance in a later chapter.

Security of payment

Following our recognition of the fact that ignorance of procedure is a prime danger to payment and results in many a loss, it is important to note that this is particularly relevant to documentary collections. I have encountered the situation a number of times over the years where an exporter, having carefully prepared a bill of exchange in the manner we have discussed, attaches the shipping documents and sends the complete set to the buyer. The effect is to reduce the security position to the minimum level associated with open account; the buyer is in possession of documents to enable clearance of goods and, if so minded, may ignore the bill received for payment or acceptance.

Security with this method of payment is achieved by using the banking system, the procedure being as follows. The exporter draws the bill of exchange and hands it, with the shipping documents, to its bank which, in this context, is termed the remitting bank. The instructions, which are given to the bank and which will be examined in detail later, include an authority to deliver the documents to the buyer only on the fulfilment of one of two conditions, namely:

1 on the buyer paying the amount of the bill of exchange. This is known as documents against payment (or D/P) and is usually the authority given in respect of sight bills only;
2 on the buyer accepting the bill of exchange for the amount thereof payable in accordance with the tenor (usance). This is known as documents against acceptance (or D/A) and is the authority always applied to usance bills.

Upon receipt of the exporter's instructions the bank will send the documents and bill of exchange to its correspondent bank in the buyer's country, which is termed the collecting bank, repeating to it the delivery instructions (D/P or D/A) as indicated by the exporter. The dispatch by the remitting bank to the collecting bank may well be in two mailings, the second containing the second of exchange (duplicate bill of exchange), if there is one, and the duplicate shipping documents, plus a copy of the remitting bank's instructions included in the first mailing.

Figure 6.1: Life cycle of a Bill of Exchange

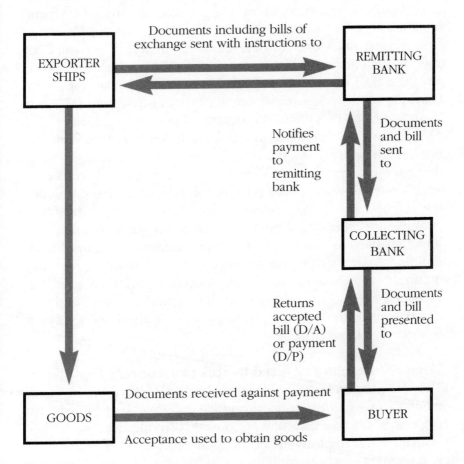

The collecting bank, on receiving documents, will present them to the buyer direct or through a local bank acting on the collecting bank's instructions; the bank is then known as the presenting bank. In either event the presentation will be in order that the buyer has an opportunity to examine the documents but during that examination they will remain under the control of the presenting bank. Only when the buyer makes payment or accepts the bill of exchange, dependent on whether the delivery instructions are D/P or D/A, will the documents be released when they can be used to obtain possession of the goods. Meanwhile the collecting bank will retain any accepted bill unless instructed to return it to the remitting bank, and will confirm that either payment or acceptance has taken place. The remitting bank will then advise the exporter accordingly. Figure 6.1 illustrates the procedure.

Thus security exists for the exporter in that the banks, as agents, will not release documents of title to the buyer until payment (D/P) or acceptance (D/A) is obtained. The importer's (buyer's) security lies in not having to make payment (D/P) or accept the bill (D/A) until documents of title are received.

At this point it is helpful to comment that a bill of exchange is not always used if payment is to be made against shipping documents. Sometimes, for example, there may be considerations, such as stamp duty payable on bills of exchange, under the regulations of the buyer's country and this may be for a prohibitive amount. If there is not a bill of exchange the remitting bank is instructed in a similar manner to that already detailed, except that the authority is to deliver documents without any reference to a bill. Where a period of credit is extended by the exporter to the buyer and the documentary collection method of payment is agreed there is always a usance bill of exchange.

What risks are not covered by this procedure?

The exporter must recognize that the banks involved in documentary collections are intermediaries only, they accept no responsibility other than that of correctly carrying out a principal's instructions. If the buyer rejects the documents on presentation it is the exporter who must face the problem of warehousing and insuring the goods in the short term and having them returned to its country unless it can find an alternative buyer. A further risk applies if the documents do not include one of title to the goods, which will be the case in respect of air, rail or road transit. Although in such an instance the buyer, having rejected the documents, may not be in a position to clear, as distinct from claim, the goods, the exporter's task in resolving the position is complicated. In some cases with the prior consent of the bank, it may be possible to consign the goods to them for release only against payment or acceptance.

The importer's main reservations concerning documentary collections must be that while the documents may be examined to ensure they describe the goods as agreed in the contract, it has no means of verifying that the goods actually dispatched are in accordance with that description until after having paid or accepted the bill. This risk also applies to the letter of credit method of payment and an importer wishing to secure protection against shipment of wrong or inferior goods should consider requesting an inspection certificate.

Instructing the bank

Exhibit 6.3 is a form of instruction – 'Foreign Bill and or Document for Collection' – for completion when an exporter requests his bank to undertake a documentary collection; the form is sometimes referred to as a bill lodgement form or a collection order. Minor variations may occur in the forms in use by individual banks but the specimen shown is an example of the type of information required. It is produced by The Simplification of International Trade Procedures Board (SITPRO) whose aim is to encourage better (and simpler) trading practices. Supported in the United Kingdom by the Department of Trade and Industry, its contribution to international trade is recognized worldwide. The collection order (exhibit 6.3) is indicative of SITPRO's concentration on clarity without the use of excessive wording and it forms the basis upon which this type of instruction is framed by the banking industry. Many of the requirements are obviously for record purposes in case of subsequent query, others self explanatory, but the following merit comment. The observations are in the same order as the relative stipulations appear on the form.

Exhibit 6.3: Foreign Bill and/or Documents for Collection

Drawer/exporter					**Lloyds Bank**	**Action Copy for UK** 64 **International Operations** ᴍ5.92
						Drawer's/exporter's reference
					We enclose documents for collection. Please follow instructions marked X.	Branch reference
Consignee name and address (note 1)					Drawee (if not consignee) name and address	
Collecting bank (if known)					To:- Lloyds Bank Plc branch	

I/WE ENCLOSE THE FOLLOWING BILL(S)/DOCUMENT(S) FOR COLLECTION BY AIRMAIL (note 2)

Bill of exchange	Commercial invoice	Certified/consular invoice	Certificate of origin	Insurance policy/ certificate	Bill of lading	Parcel post receipt	Air waybill
Combined transport document	Other documents and whereabouts of any missing original bills of lading						

Goods and carrying vessel			If unaccepted ➡ and advise reason by (note 4)		protest	do not protest
Release documents against (note3)	ACCEPTANCE	PAYMENT			teletransmission	airmail
If documents are not taken up on arrival of goods, request immediate advice by teletransmission and (note 5)	warehouse goods	do not warehouse	If unpaid ➡ and advise reason by (note 4)		protest	do not protest
	insure against fire	do not insure			teletransmission	airmail
Collect ALL charges (note 9)			Advise acceptance and due date by		teletransmission	airmail
Collect correspondent's charges only			Remit proceeds by (note 6)		teletransmission	airmail
If charges refused	waive	do not waive	If local regulations require, a deposit in local currency may be taken (note 7)			
In case of need refer to (note 8):-					for information only	
					accept their instructions without reserve	

SPECIAL INSTRUCTIONS: 1. Represent on arrival of goods if not honoured on first presentation.

This collection is subject to the I.C.C. Uniform Rules for Collections (latest revision). The choice of correspondent rests with Lloyds Bank unless specific instructions are given on this form to present through a named bank direct without the intervention of any intermediary. Unless otherwise instructed, unaccepted term bills will be sent for acceptance and, following acceptance, will be retained by the correspondent pending presentation for payment at maturity. Airmail is used wherever possible unless otherwise instructed. Duplicate documents are also sent by airmail.

Date of bill of exchange	Amount of collection	**Apply proceeds as indicated below**
Tenor		Credit sterling account number
		Credit currency account number
Bill of exchange claused:		Apply against forward contract No: F E
		Any General Letter of Hypothecation signed by me/us shall apply in connection with the above transaction. I/We agree that you shall not be held liable for any loss, damage or delay, however caused, which is not directly due to the negligence of your own officers or servants.
These instructions are confirmed		Company name, authorised signature and date
Manager, Lloyds Bank Plc	branch	

The request for the full name and address of the drawee is more important than might at first appear. True, it is normally on the bill itself but banks insist that it is also shown on the lodgement form: failure to do so may well result in the form and documents being returned for the omission to be remedied. The bank will endeavour to ascertain the address, but assumes no responsibility to do so.

Following the formal listing of documents which are included in the collection, information is sought regarding the whereabouts of any bill of lading not included. As we have seen, an important feature in the security considerations is title to the goods, and this is encompassed in the bill of lading, itself a document of title. If the bills of lading have been issued in a set – the normal practice – and one or more are missing, this may enable the buyer to obtain possession of the goods if the missing bill(s) has been sent to it by the exporter. Without a bill of lading the buyer will normally be unable to gain possession of the goods, except in the case where a banker's indemnity has been given to the shipping company. If the bank has no interest in the transaction, beyond acting as the remitting bank in the collection procedure, the question may be asked for recording purposes only, in case of subsequent enquiry or dishonour of the bill with a consequent need to protect the exporter's interests, although it is also an implicit warning to the exporter that a document of title is absent from the collection.

If the bank has agreed to provide finance against the collection, either by way of an advance or through negotiating the bill, both of which will be discussed further in chapter 10, the question assumes greater importance to the bank in its own right. It may well have taken into account the value of the goods in agreeing to assist the exporter, and will wish to be assured that the security thereby achieved will not be lost by the goods being released to the buyer against the missing bill of lading.

The lower portion of the form contains a number of instructions over and above the principal one for releasing documents against acceptance of payment. We will deal first with those concerning the position in the unfortunate event of the bill being dishonoured; that is, the buyer (drawee) refuses payment against a sight bill or to accept a usance bill. If this occurs two

125

areas for immediate decision in the exporter's interests arise. The first is what action is to be taken regarding the dishonoured bill, the second is the avoidance of the situation where the goods have not been claimed on arrival and substantial demurrage charges (the term applied to costs claimed by the port authorities at the place of discharge for unclaimed goods) are in prospect.

You will remember earlier reference to the concern of some buyers that the documentary collection, while ensuring that the documents are released immediately on payment or acceptance, does not provide an opportunity for examining the goods until after these events. The form therefore contains provision for the exporter, if willing, to authorize the bank in the event of dishonour on first presentation to re-present on arrival of the goods. Clearly, if this course of action is approved no other measures need be adopted in respect of the initial dishonour, but will be reconsidered should the documents not be taken up on arrival of the goods.

If there is no provision for re-presentation or upon such re-presentation the bill is again dishonoured, the form allows the exporter to instruct the bank to 'protest' the bill. 'Protest' and the less formal act of 'noting' are procedures which the holder of a dishonoured bill of exchange must follow to protect its rights to pursue the drawee. The procedures are also normally subject to a time limit and this is one reason for the bank seeking instructions in advance. The time in which protest must be made, and indeed whether the procedure can be adopted and if so the legal significance, vary from country to country. An exporter may well wish to take legal advice before deciding on the instruction to be given to the bank unless familiar with the situation through previous experience.

For details of the procedures the reader should refer to the companion book in this series, *Principles of Law Relating to Overseas Trade*. Sufficient for our purposes is to observe that the collecting bank will in the event of dishonour, and if so instructed by the remitting bank, request a notary public to re-present the bill and prepare a written document, 'the protest', evidencing the dishonour drawn up in whatsoever form, shall be acceptable to enable action in a court of law in the country concerned. The act of protest is considered sufficiently vital (in its absence legal rights may be lost) that banks' lodgement forms require exporters to indicate if the process is **not** to be followed on dishonour.

You may well be thinking that this is a very involved matter for the exporter to evaluate, particularly if exporting to a wide selection of markets, each of which may have different legal provisions on dishonour and protesting. Of course you are perfectly correct, and for that reason many exporters will appoint a 'case of need', often their commercial agent, in overseas countries. This individual or firm may be better placed than the exporter to judge the best course of action and additionally has the advantage of proximity to the problem. Observe that the form requires the powers of any case of need to be clearly defined; either it or they are purely a source of information, probably to be relayed back to the exporter to assist in his evaluation, or the bank is empowered to take instructions 'without reserve'. It is this latter option which underlines the care which the exporter must exercise in selecting a case of need. If instructions are accepted without reserve they may include one to release the documents without payment or acceptance of the bill, the very core of documentary collection procedure, and to countenance such a possibility the exporter must have complete faith in his 'case of need'.

Consider now the second danger consequent upon dishonour; that the goods will arrive, remain unclaimed and attract substantial demurrage (compensation for delay). To meet this situation the bank seeks instructions from the exporter regarding warehousing and insurance. The former is not always possible although desirable, the latter is essential and, if the bank has an interest, it will insist on insurance. Once again this is emphasized by its insistence that the exporter specifically indicates if insurance is **not** to be arranged. You will, incidentally, appreciate that the transit insurance will be terminated on arrival of the goods or, if their intended onward journey is frustrated, at that point and this is the reason action must be taken to re-insure in the new circumstances. The form particularly specifies the risk of fire and requires the exporter to state if it is, or is not, to be covered. However the exporter may choose to nominate other risks under 'special instructions' dependent upon the circumstances and the nature of the goods.

Returning to our intention of commenting on the speed achievable under each method of payment, that for documentary collections is normally quicker than for open account but slower than under a documentary letter of credit. However, much can be done to accelerate collections where amounts warrant if the form is completed with care and thought. In three instances the exporter is asked how communication should be effected between the collecting and remitting bank; advice of acceptance, remittance of proceeds and advice of non-payment or non-acceptance. In each case the choice lies between fax, telex, cable and airmail. Exporters will make their decision on remittance according to the criteria laid down under open account: the amount and interest rates prevailing. On acceptance airmail will probably suffice unless the exporter is apprehensive and seeks peace of mind. Where dishonour takes place I would advise cable advice, as speed is essential in following up, unless a case of need has been given power to act without reserve where airmail might suffice although even in such instances it is important the credit controller is aware of the dishonour at the earliest possible time.

Note the wording of the instruction at the foot of the form – 'Please collect the above mentioned bill and/or documents'. This confirms the earlier comment that where no bill is used the collection procedures are unaltered.

If all charges are not to be borne by the exporter the form should be completed in the appropriate boxes to indicate that all charges or the correspondent bank charges only are to be collected from the drawee. However the buyer may refuse a request to meet such charges and, were the collecting bank to insist on payment, may refuse payment of both charges **and principal**. For this reason banks will normally waive charges if refused unless the exporter stipulates 'charges may not be waived' on the collection order. This is further illustration of the importance of exporters and buyers coming to a firm agreement on charges at the time the contract of sale is concluded.

In their adaptation of the Sitpro Foreign Bill and/or Documents for Collection Form, individual banks may include various additions. Among these are the ability of the exporter to use the same form to cover bills of exchange which are to be negotiated by the bank (immediate finance is being sought as distinct from the exporter awaiting the proceeds of collection). This option is achieved by adding to the choice between 'collection' and 'acceptance and collection' (indicating that the bill of exchange after acceptance is to be held by the collecting bank and presented on maturity) a third option: 'negotiation'.

Some banks also make provision in the form for the exporter to give instructions regarding the disposal of foreign currency proceeds of collection. The options in that event are:

1 in sterling converted at the spot rate of exchange;
2 by credit to a foreign currency account in the exporter's name; or
3 to apply the proceeds to fulfil delivery requirements under a Forward Exchange Contract (see chapter 4).

The clausing of bills of exchange

In examining the bank lodgement form you may have noticed that in the particulars of the bill of exchange which are listed, reference is made to clauses which may appear and must be drawn to the bank's attention. There are a variety of clauses but, remembering our definition of a bill and the implications regarding its being drawn in a correct form, no clause may contain a condition on the payment, and clauses can only clarify the amount payable as regards amount or rate of exchange in order to avoid misunderstandings. The following are examples of common clauses preceded by a statement of the circumstances in which they arise and the purpose they are intended to fulfil. All the clauses concerning rates of exchange would normally appear only on sterling bills; remember chapter 4 where we observed that with a currency bill it was the exporter's risk and it is responsible for the foreign exchange deal necessary to produce sterling. However a bill drawn on a buyer not in the currency of his country but in a third currency which was subsequently to be converted into sterling by the exporter, for example a Peruvian buyer on whom the exporter has drawn in US Dollars, might be claused to indicate the rate of exchange to be applied in converting from local currency to US Dollars.

1 The exporter wishes to receive the face amount of the sterling bill less collection and stamp charges which it has agreed to pay – 'Payable at the collecting bank's current rate of exchange for demand drafts on London . . .'

2 The exporter wishes to receive the face amount of the sterling bill plus collection charges and stamp duty – 'Payable at the collecting bank's current rate of exchange for demand drafts on London together with all bank charges and stamps.'

3 The exporter has agreed with the buyer that the latter will pay interest at a stated rate while the bill is in course of collection (this would normally assume that the exporter is being financed and seeks reimbursement) – 'Payable at the collecting bank's current rate of exchange for demand drafts on London plus interest at 9 per cent per annum from the date hereof until the approximate arrival of remittance in London together with all bank charges and stamps.' This clause can be used for either a sight or usance bill.

There are many variations on the above wordings and, provided the intention is clear, they would be acceptable; for example, in place of, 'collecting bank's current rate of exchange for demand drafts on London', the clause could read: 'collecting bank's selling rate for telegraphic transfers on London.' One must, however, stress once again that the clausing must be agreed between exporter and buyer, and if there is any doubt as to the technical accuracy of a bank's procedural practice a banker's agreement should also be requested.

A small but practical point on interest. It is always preferable, having received the buyer's agreement, to clause the bill rather than to ask for the payment of the interest under 'other instructions' on the lodgement form. The latter raises questions in the minds of the banks as to whether the addition may be an afterthought and poses the problem of what action is to be taken in the event of the buyer refusing the interest; is the capital sum to be sacrificed through refusal? By clausing the bill the interest element becomes an integral part of the instrument and there is no question of refusing interest; the bill is paid or refused for the complete sum.

Direct collections

We have noted the dangers of goods arriving before documents, with the consequent payment of demurrage charges; the constant shortening of sea journeys aggravates this problem. The time element in processing a documentary collection includes delivery by the exporter's account-holding branch to their foreign or international branch, the period taken for dispatch by that branch to their correspondent bank in the buyer's country (the collecting bank), and processing by that bank, including presentation to the buyer. To endeavour to solve the problem by the exporter sending a negotiable copy of the bill of lading direct to the buyer or in the ship's bag will, as we have seen, destroy the security enjoyed by the exporter under the documentary collection method of payment, namely that documents of title to the goods will not be released other than against payment or acceptance of the bill.

Another possible solution is to have the goods consigned to the collecting bank who may then arrange clearance but this answer also has disadvantages. It may only be used if the prior consent of the bank is obtained and, in these days when banks are very cost-conscious and therefore reluctant to offer services which are both labour intensive and peripheral to their main functions, they may well decline to act. Even if they do agree, the charges incurred for their services and those of the forwarding agents they employ may be not only substantial but also a source of contention between exporter and buyer as to amount and liability.

A third option used in circumstances where a reasonable degree of trust exists between buyer and seller is the Seaway Bill (also known as a Waybill, Shipping Company's Waybill or Liner Waybill). This document is a receipt for the goods, is non-negotiable and enables the consignee to take possession of the goods without having to produce a document of title. For the reasons given earlier, banks will be reluctant to provide finance against documents including a Seaway Bill if they are seeking an element of security in the goods themselves.

As an attempt to provide some shortening of the documentary collection procedure, some banks have introduced a service enabling customers to send the collection direct to the correspondent bank in the buyer's country, thus reducing the time schedule, perhaps by several days. Not a great saving, but often decisive in documents arriving before the goods. The direct relationship between the exporter and the collecting bank is confined to the act of transmitting documents, thereafter the bank will deal with the collection exactly as if it had been received from the remitting bank advising it of the fate of the bill and sending proceeds directly. The exporter using this system, which is rapidly expanding, completes a collection schedule addressed to the correspondent bank; the information contained being very similar to that called for in the bank lodgement form discussed earlier.

Uniform Rules for Collection

In chapter 3 praise was accorded to the International Chamber of Commerce for instigating 'Incoterms', an internationally accepted clarification of delivery terms. Similar thanks are due to the Chamber for drawing up a code of practice for parties involved in dealing with collections, both clean and documentary, which has been adopted in the United Kingdom by the British Bankers' Association and the Accepting Houses Committee. The code is also widely accepted internationally and, as will have been noticed on our specimen lodgement form, collections subject to the terms of Uniform Rules for Collection are suitably annotated.

Interested readers, including those studying for the examinations of The Institute of Export, should obtain copies of the code from:

ICC Publishing SA,
38 Cours Albert 1er,

75008 Paris,
France

or through any of the ICC National Committees, which for the United Kingdom is at:

14/15 Belgrave Square,
London,
SW1X 8PS.
Publication number 322.

The following comments on some of the more important articles in the rules as regards exporters' viewpoints may be helpful if read in conjunction with the following articles.

General provisions and definitions

Following a definition of terms, most of which we have already covered, this section ends with a stipulation which is comforting to the exporter wrestling for the first time with documentary collection procedures. It requires a bank which is unable for any reason to comply with instructions its customer has included in the collection order (lodgement form) immediately to advise the customer of that inability. Perhaps obvious but nevertheless reassuring, this provision should not, however, be taken as a reason for lack of care in preparing the lodgement form; if the bank has to return it, valuable time in presentation is lost.

Article 2

An important article, the implications of which are not always appreciated, it limits the obligations of the bank in examining documents presented under cover of a lodgement form to verifying that the documents actually received appear to be in accordance with the listing in the form. Should this not be the case the party completing the form must be advised immediately. The implied warning to exporters is that, contrary to the belief of many, the bank is under no obligation to check shipping documents for such obvious mistakes as the absence of dating, a failure to sign or authenticate a signature, or a variance between documents in the description of goods or shipping marks. The bank may, and often does, give a superficial check and draw the exporter's attention to such errors or omissions as a service to its customer, but it is not bound to do so and will accept no responsibility if the errors pass unnoticed and cause problems or expense in clearing the goods.

Article 3

This article mentions that the exporter may nominate the collecting bank to be utilized, but if no nomination is made the remitting bank may make the choice. Exporters would not normally nominate but, on occasion, the buyer may request them to do so. In considering such a request it must be remembered that, while the remitting bank will comply with any nomination, the consequences in the event of additional delay or extra costs arising are the responsibility of the exporter as orderer.

Article 6

Underlines the caution mentioned earlier in this chapter against consigning goods to a bank **without first obtaining its consent** by reminding exporters that, should this be done, the bank is not obliged to take delivery of the goods which will then remain the responsibility of the shipper. Surely an excellent reason for extreme care.

Article 9

By stressing what is perhaps common sense, that the presenting bank must make presentation for payment or acceptance without delay, the article indicates that banks are aware of the need for urgency.

Article 12

Contains a safeguard against an exporter being paid in a local currency which is not fully convertible, despite the bill being expressed in sterling or another convertible currency. The bank is required to release documents only against payment of the currency of the bill which is available for immediate remittance in the terms of the instructions in the lodgement form. In circumstances where, exceptionally, exporter and buyer have agreed that local currency is acceptable or perhaps mandatory as a prelude to foreign exchange being allocated, the lodgement form may specifically authorize this to take place and provision for such an exception to the normal course is made in the article.

Articles 15 and 16

Although the presenting bank is responsible for ensuring any acceptance if a bill 'appears to be complete and correct', it is not responsible for the authenticity of any signature or for the capacity of any signatory to sign. This provision is understandable if one considers the effects of the delay which would ensue if the bank were to be responsible for verifying these matters.

Article 19

This article embodies the principle that in documentary collections the banks involved have no obligations in respect of the underlying goods. In the event of being so instructed on the lodgement form it will take action to protect goods in case of dishonour of the bill and may entrust other parties with implementation. It may, in the absence of instructions, take similar action, but the important fact is that it takes no responsibility for the fate or condition of the goods or for the acts or omissions of third parties. If action is taken it must be advised promptly to the remitting bank for transmission to the exporter who will be accountable for the charges and expenses incurred.

7

Documentary Credits: Obtaining the Credit

The methods of payment considered up to this point – payment in advance, open account and documentary collections – have a common factor, the exporter relies on the buyer for payment. True, in the case of documentary collections there is an inducement on the buyer to settle in that it will not obtain documents of title to the goods unless it does so, but there is no other source of payment to which the exporter may turn. The involvement of the banks in these methods, whether as remitters or recipients of the funds in settlement or in handling documentation, is as intermediaries with no responsibility or guarantee that the payment will be made.

We turn now to a method of payment under which a bank (or banks) stands between exporter and buyer not just as a convenient medium through which funds may be passed, but with a clearly defined responsibility for payment. The exporter is no longer obliged to look **solely** to the buyer for settlement. For this reason the documentary letter of credit is the most secure method of payment and, while used across a wide range of circumstances where choice exists, is the only prudent method when a financial report on a buyer specifies 'dealings recommended on a secured basis'.

The documentary credit is also a flexible instrument which can meet the needs of a variety of situations provided the correct type of credit is used. The skill we seek is to identify the correct type for any particular set of circumstances. With this in mind the description of each type in this chapter will be followed by details of the sort of situation in which it is best used and warnings on any needs it will not cover. First however the broad concept of a credit must be understood – what exactly the instrument represents.

The Definition of a Letter of Credit

In international trade we are concerned with documentary as distinct from clean letters of credit but to avoid any possible confusion we will note that a clean letter of credit is a means by which one bank authorizes another to make payments to its customer and guarantees reimbursement up to an agreed amount. For example if you were visiting an overseas country and staying in a major city with a conveniently placed local bank for your monetary needs you might, as an alternative to carrying foreign currency or travellers cheques, request your bank to authorize the local bank to cash your cheques up to a fixed amount. If your bank agreed the authority they would issue what is known as a 'clean credit' or an 'open credit'. A documentary credit is an undertaking given in writing by a bank to the addressee (beneficiary), who is normally the exporter, to make payment within the expiry date of the credit against the presentation of documents which conform to the terms of the credit (which will specify the documents required thereunder) and the conditions stipulated therein.

It is not therefore an **unconditional** guarantee of payment but a guarantee which is **conditional**. The bill of exchange which is normally called for under a documentary credit and which is drawn on the bank can be at sight or usance and the credit is therefore equally appropriate in covering sales requiring settlement after an agreed period or those requiring immediate settlement. If the bill is for, say, 120 days sight and the presentation is in order the bank will accept and, as we shall observe when considering methods of finance, the accepted bank bill then becomes an extremely useful means of raising money at a fine rate of interest.

Opening a Documentary Credit

There are four parties to a documentary credit:

1 **The opener** (also termed the applicant or accountee) is the buyer who instructs the bank to open a letter of credit. When it has done so, it becomes:
2 **the opening (or issuing) bank** and forwards the credit to its correspondents in the exporting country who become:
3 **the advising bank** when it advises the credit to the:
4 **beneficiary** (exporter).

In detail the actions leading up to the opening will follow a pattern which commences with the quotation for the sale of goods. This will establish the delivery terms and, in consequence, the documentation required by the buyer together with the requirement that payment is to be made through a documentary letter of credit. Further communication between exporter and buyer will have agreed any additional details regarding the documentation.

The buyer will approach his bank requesting that the credit be opened and specifying the type which will also have been discussed and agreed between exporter and buyer. At this point we see an immediate result of the direct involvement of the bank in the payment chain; as it will be giving its own conditional undertaking to pay it naturally regards the opening of the credit as being a facility granted to its customer, the opener. If that customer should fail to reimburse the bank at a later stage for payments correctly made under the credit, the bank, who will have honoured its undertaking, will sustain a loss. Thus the liability will be considered against the customer's financial standing and, if thought appropriate, additional security will be sought over and above the value of the goods which will normally be pledged to the bank and sold if reimbursement is not forthcoming.

When asking for a letter of credit exporters should realise that the buyer, if agreeing, is utilizing its bank facilities in opening the credit. A further liability for the buyer may arise in certain countries where a shortage of foreign exchange results in regulations requiring importers to pay all or a proportion of the credit amount by way of deposit when the credit is opened. This is designed to restrict imports but is a considerable financial burden for the opener. In addition to liability provisions the opening bank will satisfy itself that any import regulations relating to the goods have been obeyed and any necessary licences obtained.

When satisfied on all these matters the opening bank will issue the documentary credit forwarding it to the advising bank which will, in turn, convey it to the beneficiary (exporter).

The Main Categories of Documentary Credits

There are three main categories, namely: revocable, irrevocable and irrevocable and confirmed.

Revocable credits

This is the least desirable category and the security to the exporter is prejudiced by the ability of the buyer at any time to instruct the opening bank to cancel. Upon receipt by the advising bank of such notice of cancellation it is no longer able to accept presentation of documents and the exporter is left to try to obtain redress against the buyer. Obviously a revocable credit is an open invitation to a dishonest buyer receiving an offer of similar goods at a lower price to renege on the original deal by instructing the opening bank to revoke. Exporters should not only refuse revocable credits when offered as a means of payment but also check any documentary credit received in response to requests for irrevocable credit to make certain it does not state the undertaking to be revocable. We shall see, when considering in chapter 8 the rules on the interpretation of the vast majority of documentary credits (known as Uniform Customs and Practice for Documentary Credits) that the 1993 revision *UCP 500* in force from 1 January 1994 states that, in the absence of any indication of revocability, a documentary credit is assumed to be irrevocable. The previous 1983 revision, in contrast, had stated that the reverse was true – that unless there was an indication of irrevocability a credit was assumed to be revocable. Remember that for some time after the Ist January 1994 there will be Letters of Credit in circulation which may be subject to either UCP (the 1983 revision) 400 or UCP 500, dependent on which is quoted in the individual credit as the governing rules, and great care will be necessary in examination of the wording.

Revocable credits are rarely seen except in certain trades where they are traditionally used for convenience despite the fact that exporter and buyer have complete confidence in each other and would, without doubt, have dealt willingly on open account terms.

Irrevocable credits

The improvement in security for the exporter when an irrevocable documentary credit is offered in comparison with the revocable variety is significant. The irrevocable credit, as its name suggests, carries the irrevocable undertaking of the opening bank that it will make payment against documents presented which comply with the terms of the credit provided presentation is made within the validity date. This assurance is moreover bolstered by the fact that no amendment can be made to the credit terms unless agreed by all parties including the exporter (beneficiary). In many cases such a credit is wholly acceptable to an exporter but the point must be made that the undertaking is only as strong as the opening bank.

Leading banks throughout the world would normally be considered acceptable as credit openers but in some countries there exists a profusion of small banks – some of which have only a few or even a single branch. It is customary for these banks to be predominantly domestically oriented, often with activities confined to a particular industry, in which they specialize, and any international business they are asked to undertake is done through a larger and more internationally experienced correspondent bank in their own country. Sometimes a documentary credit may be issued by a small bank and the amount for which it is opened may represent a substantial percentage of the opening bank's assets with the attendant risk. If such a credit is routed through an advising bank there is no obligation on that bank to consider the standing of the opening bank unless it agrees to negotiate and therefore seek reimbursement. Although the likelihood of the exporter receiving a credit of this nature is very small it does illustrate that an enquiry to its bank on the standing of the opening bank could be desirable in case of doubt.

The only other reason for hesitating to accept an irrevocable credit from a bank outside the exporter's country is associated with country risk which we examined in detail in chapter 2. A situation which has actually occurred is always preferable to an imagined scenario when illustrating a principle. Just such a situation can be quoted in citing circumstances when a credit irrevocable by an overseas bank of good standing is rendered ineffective due to country risk. The Suez Canal crisis in the 1950s resulted in the Egyptian Authorities freezing British assets in Egypt and the United Kingdom took similar action in respect of Egyptian assets in this country. At the time of the crisis many United Kingdom exporters held letters of credit issued by first class Egyptian banks, covering exports to that country, and those credits were irrevocable on the part of the issuing bank.

However, when documents were presented to the United Kingdom advising banks, who would normally have been prepared to negotiate, they were refused payment despite being in compliance with the credit terms. The reason for non-payment was that the United Kingdom banks were unable to reimburse themselves by debiting their Egyptian Bank principal's account due to the freezing of funds and as advising banks only they had no obligation to pay the beneficiaries (exporters) who had to await an end to the crisis before seeking payment. Some exporters at that time were, notwithstanding the political situation, able to obtain payment being in possession of irrevocable and confirmed credits.

Irrevocable and confirmed credits

This term is applied to a credit which bears not only the irrevocable undertaking of the opening bank but also a second undertaking (confirmation) in identical terms from a bank which is normally situated in the exporter's country. That bank which is again the correspondent of the opening bank then becomes the 'confirming bank' in place of its previous title of 'advising bank', when it assumed no obligation in its own right to make payment. The reason confirming banks in the United Kingdom made payment during the Suez crisis, despite being unable to claim reimbursement until it was over, was that it would have been unthinkable for them to have failed to fulfil their undertaking as this would have been highly detrimental to their international standing.

The lesson for exporters today is that where country risk is high it is the irrevocable credit confirmed by a United Kingdom bank which should be sought. The use of the phrase 'confirmed by a United Kingdom bank' as distinct from 'confirmed by a bank in the United Kingdom' is quite deliberate and emphasizes a distinction which is not always apparent to the unsuspecting exporter. There are, in this country, many branches or representative offices of banks domiciled abroad and exporters might be offered letters of credit purporting to be 'confirmed' by those offices. While the term 'confirmed' may be used in a variety of ways, for example in the context of authentication, in regard to letters of credit it is quite specifically applied to a second bank – normally in the exporter's country – which has added its undertaking to that of the opening bank. A moment's thought will reveal that if the opening bank has given its undertaking and its United Kingdom branch has done likewise the exporter has in essence one bank only to whom it may look for payment and that bank is not domiciled in the United Kingdom.

Unfortunately for exporters it is not always possible to obtain a confirmed credit even if the buyer appears content that settlement should be made in that manner. The reasons may not always be apparent. In some countries there is a strong sense of nationalism which manifests itself in an extreme reluctance to request banks abroad to confirm letters of credit, regarding it almost as a 'slight' on their indigenous banks to do so. This may however be reluctantly overcome if the goods being imported are vital to the national economy. In other cases banks approached with a request to confirm may not be willing to do so and will indicate that fact to the opening bank but the exporter is obviously unaware of this exchange. The unwillingness may result from the standing of the opening bank but much more frequently it is due to the country risk. Here a word on the bank to bank considerations may be helpful.

A clearing bank in the United Kingdom and its counterpart in other countries will receive many requests for confirmation from a variety of countries with different international credit standings. It will have decided the maximum amount of credit which, with reasonable prudence, it should make available to each country dependent upon the risk involved and a part of that credit will be available as 'lines' or 'limits' to banks in the country which are asking for their credits to be confirmed. The liability of the confirming bank is real since having given its undertaking it must pay notwithstanding any difficulty in recovering from the opening bank. The extent to which the limit is utilized will vary from day to day with new requests to confirm being received but existing credits expiring or being paid, but if the limit becomes fully utilized the bank extending the facility will refuse any further requests to confirm.

Another aspect not always clear to the exporter is that because the limit for confirming credits is extended to the opening bank it is that and that alone which may request confirmation be given to any particular credit. Exporters often request buyers to arrange for credits to be advised through or confirmed by the exporter's own bank. Although the opening bank may not comply with such a request received from the opener, perhaps because it has no correspondent relationship with the bank concerned, it is a sensible plea to the buyer as it is always easier to deal with one's own bank particularly if difficulties arise. This does not however include, as some exporters wrongly imagine, the ability to obtain a degree of preference in having a credit confirmed; the confirming bank will normally have no control over which credits are submitted for confirmation under a limit except perhaps when two identical credits are received at the same time only one of which can be accommodated within the limit.

Letters of credit have the advantage of security as we have seen and are also the speediest method of settlement after payment in advance, as the exporter can submit shipping documents **in the United Kingdom** immediately they are received. They are also the most expensive method and this is particularly so in the case of confirmed credits. The confirmation commission which – together with the opening, amendment and negotiation (payment) commissions – makes up the cost, varies according to the country in which the opening bank is domiciled.

'Country exposure' is a term applied by banks to the amount of facilities they allow to a country and where the country risk is high this 'exposure' is a very scarce commodity and in consequence commands a high price (or commission). The cost of a credit is borne by the opener unless otherwise agreed but it is quite usual for the exporter requiring a credit to agree to contribute. Occasionally the exporter will meet all charges but it is much more common for costs to be split with the opener meeting the banking charges incurred in its country and the exporter those which are levied by the United Kingdom bank including confirming commission. It is important therefore in cases of scarce exposure for the exporter to ascertain the likely amount of such charges before accepting any obligation to defray them.

Reference is sometimes made to the possibility of exporters obtaining a silent confirmation to a letter of credit. This seemingly odd description derives from a departure from the normal situation where the buyer's bank is naturally aware that the credit has been confirmed and was in fact responsible for the instruction that this be done. To be precise a silent confirmation is not a confirmation in the sense we have been discussing thus far. It is a separate undertaking which a bank in the exporter's country might give that, in the event of documents in compliance with the terms being presented under an irrevocable letter of credit opened by a bank in the buyer's country being unpaid, they will make payment in lieu. The undertaking has equal effect so far as the exporter is concerned to that of the normal confirmation but its existence is unknown to the opening bank or the buyer.

Such undertakings are not easily obtainable and have the same scarcity value in relation to credits opened by high risk countries as normal confirmations. They are not related to limits given to banks abroad and may be offered entirely at the discretion of the bank concerned based on individual circumstances, thereby offering considerable flexibility. They may also demonstrate the fact that some banks which have historical links with particular countries or areas overseas are naturally under pressure to extend lines to their correspondent banks to the maximum possible, commensurate with prudence, while others may have few traditional associations and, in consequence, be prepared and able to take some risk under silent confirmations.

Instructions to banks

Of course it is the buyer, not the exporter, who instructs the bank to open a documentary credit but it is greatly in the exporter's interests that those instructions are correct. It is possible to amend an irrevocable credit with the consent of all parties but it can be expensive; it is much more desirable that this should not be necessary.

Exhibit 7.1 is a specimen application to open a documentary credit, required by one of the United Kingdom clearing banks and is basically representative of the type of information which would be called for by the buyer's bank. Let us consider those requirements which are not self-explanatory and the implications as regards the information to be supplied by the exporter to the buyer before completion of the form. The order in which comments are made corresponds to that in which instruction requirements appear. The notes referred to in the form are either covered by the comments or elsewhere in this chapter.

The applicant may ask for an irrevocable **and transferable** credit to be established. The term transferable allows the beneficiary to transfer all or part of the credit to one or more other parties (second beneficiaries), and is expanded in greater detail in 'Types of documentary credit' later in this chapter.

The expiry date is the last date upon which documents may be presented to a bank at the place of expiry. That date may also be the latest shipment date but an earlier shipment date is

Exhibit 7.1: Application to Open a Documentary Letter of Credit

10/10.93 99D

	Bank Use Only
Lloyds Bank — Application to open a Documentary Letter of Credit	
Please complete in triplicate in typescript or ballpoint pen in BLOCK CAPITALS, forward the original and duplicate to the Bank and RETAIN part 3. Where applicable boxes should be marked X. Guidance notes are on the back sheet which can be detached for ease of reference.	Action Copy for for UKIO Processing Area

1. To: Lloyds Bank Plc   (Branch)

2. Please issue a Documentary Letter of Credit which is to be:
   □ Irrevocable   □ Irrevocable and Transferable   *(Note 1)*
                          □ Please request Advising Bank to Add its Confirmation   *(Note 2)*

3. Applicant's name and address   4. Beneficiary's name and address

5. Currency and Amount (in figures and words)

6. Available with: *(Note 3)*
   either □ Lloyds Bank in UK by   □ sight payment   □ acceptance   □ deferred payment
   or □ Advising Bank by   □ sight payment   □ acceptance   □ negotiation   □ deferred payment
   or □ Any Bank by negotiation ('freely negotiable')

7. Drafts:
   Please read *Note 4* before marking one of these boxes.
   □ Drafts required   □ Drafts not required
   [ ] Drafts at beneficiary's option

8. If to be available on a Usance basis
   either [ ]   days sight
   or   [ ]   days after date of
   or   [ ] Other

9. Expiry Date
   in   (Country) *(Note 5)*

10. Shipment/Dispatch from
    to   latest   *(Note 6)*

11. Presentation Period   days after shipment date
    as evidenced by the Transport document   *(Note 7)*

12. Partial Shipment
    □ Allowed □ Prohibited

13. Transhipment *(Note 8)*
    □ Allowed □ Prohibited

14. Brief Goods Description   *(Note 9)*

15. Price Basis:
    Port or place:
    (Note 10)

16. Documents Required: If either the wording shown below is not as required, or additional documents are to be called for, please detail your precise requirements in section 19.
    □ Commercial invoice and   copies   □ Packing list and   copies   □ Certificate of origin and   copies
    □ Insurance policy/certificate in negotiable form for CIF/CIP invoice value plus   per cent covering   risks
    □ Insurance will be covered by ourselves   *(Note 11)*

17. Transport Document   *(Note 12)*
    □ Full set (or   ) clean 'on board' marine bills of lading issued 'to order' and blank endorsed covering port-to-port   *(Note 13)*
    shipment. If any of the following transport documents are required please complete consignee details.
    □ Non-negotiable 'on board' sea waybill   □ Multimodal Transport Document
    □ Air Transport Document   □ Road Transport Document   □ Forwarder's Receipt
    showing consignee as (name and address)

18. Transport Document to be Marked   □ Freight paid   □ Freight collect
    □ Notify (name and address)

19. Other Documents (if any)

20. Additional Instructions (if any)   *(Note 14)*

21. Charges   ourselves   beneficiary
    Lloyds Bank charges in the UK payable by   □   □
    Other bank charges payable by   □   □
    Reimbursing bank charges (if any) payable by □   □

22. When Effecting Payment (*see 'C' below*)
    either □ debit my/our sterling/currency account number ▢▢▢▢▢▢▢
    □ at Lloyds Bank's prevailing rate
    □ against Forward Contract number
    Maturing   rate
    or □ (other - please specify)

A. The documents and the goods and all proceeds of sale and of insurance, and all our rights as unpaid sellers, shall be pledged to you and be security to you for all obligations and liabilities incurred by you or your correspondents in connection with the Credit and for all disbursements in connection with the goods (which we hereby authorise you to pay for our account) and, to the fullest extent permitted by law, all our other liabilities to you present and future.

B. We will keep the goods fully insured and in the event of our failing to do so you may (but shall not be obliged to) insure the goods at your discretion and at our expense, and you may debit our account with the cost of so doing.

C. You may on payment debit our account with all sums paid in connection with the Credit or the goods and any commission and interest, or at any time if you think fit with the whole or part of the amount of the Credit. We will place you in funds on demand to meet such debits and at latest three days before the due date (or earlier if required by you) to meet any acceptances. In the case of Credits in foreign currency you may, unless you have agreed other settlement arrangements with us, pass any such debits in sterling at your rate of exchange ruling when you pass such debit or, if passed after payment, at your rate ruling when you receive advice of payment.
In the event of default you may at any time (whether before or after arrival) sell the documents or goods and you may debit our account with any shortfall.
We will indemnify you against all claims, demands, costs, charges and expenses which may be brought or preferred against you or which you may incur arising out of or in connection with the Credit unless directly due to your negligence or default.

D. Your rights against us shall not be affected by, and you and/or your correspondents shall not be responsible for, any loss or damage to the goods however or wherever caused, their quantity,

quality or condition or their detention by any person for whatever reason, the loss, validity, sufficiency, genuineness or accuracy of the shipping, insurance or any other documents or failure for any reason by you, your correspondents or any other person to store, protect or insure the goods, and all acts and omissions of the drawers and/or vendors and/or your correspondents and/or any other person shall be at our risk.

E. We will sign or execute and deliver any transfer, deed or other document which you may reasonably require from us to obtain possession of or perfect your title to the goods and/or to deliver the goods or vest the goods in any purchaser(s) from you, or otherwise for the recovery of any proceeds of sale or insurance.

F. If the Credit is irrevocable it may be cancelled by you at any time, but cancellation by you shall be without prejudice to our respective obligations as regards any bills negotiated or accepted or payments made thereunder or (where the credit is available by deferred payment) documents taken up before notice of such cancellation has been received at the place where the Credit is available.

G. All teletransmission messages in connection with the Credit shall be despatched at our risk and cost and (save where it is directly due to your negligence or default) you shall not be responsible for any loss caused by mistakes, mutilations or omissions in their transmission, coding or decoding or interpretation when received or by delay on the part of the teletransmission companies and/or their operators.

H. If two or more parties sign this document the obligations hereunder are joint and several.

I. This Credit is to be subject to the "Uniform Customs and Practice for Documentary Credits", 1993 Revision, International Chamber of Commerce Publication No. 500.

Lloyds Bank Plc is registered in England no 2065
Registered office: 71 Lombard Street, London EC3P 3BS
Member of IMRO and the Banking Ombudsman Scheme.
A signatory to the Code of Banking Practice.

23. Signature(s) of Applicant   24. Date
    (as per Bank Mandate)

often inserted to allow time for presentation by expiry. The exporter should investigate time schedules for sailings and the completion of supporting documentation, as appropriate, in order that the buyer can be made aware of practicable dates for both shipment and expiry.

The credit may expire in either the buyer's or the exporter's country. Most exporters will wish to negotiate documents within their own country and should therefore request the buyer to ask for expiry to be in that country. A negotiating (nominated) bank may be specified but many credits are freely negotiable, that means that any bank is a nominated bank.

If drafts are to be drawn on the advising bank, interest will be charged to the opener from the date of payment until that upon which reimbursement is made to the opening bank.

The various options for which drafts may be drawn are enumerated and a further choice is permitted whereby drafts may be omitted and payment made on deferred terms. The choice is to meet the problem mentioned earlier (in relation to documentary collections) of countries imposing prohibitive stamp duties on bills.

The block capitals used in the word 'BRIEF' (description of goods) are to emphasize that no useful purpose is achieved by including in a letter of credit a detailed description; quite the opposite: such a description may well cause difficulties in payment, as we shall observe later. A documentary credit is a contractual relationship between bank(s), exporters and buyers based solely on documents. The banks are in no way concerned with the contract of sale between exporter and buyer or with whether or not goods have been shipped in accordance with that contract. If, for example, documents are presented purporting to cover a shipment of diesel engines and being in order are paid, whereas the cases on arrival are found to contain rocks, there is no come-back to the banks. The importer seeking protection against inferior or non-existent goods should request an inspection certificate. A detailed description on the form gives no such protection and would be better if substituted by 'goods as per pro-forma invoice 1749 dated 1st December 1993'.

The price basis indicated should be consistent with the documents called for in the credit; this point was stressed in chapter 3 when we were considering the quotation.

The list of documents required under a credit can vary from a single invoice to copious documentation. The credit is not concerned with the method of dispatch selected or the completion of individual documents except in so far as they are included in the credit stipulations which must be complied with. Companion books in this series will deal with various and important considerations in relation to the purpose and suitability of transportation documents for the physical distribution of goods; we are simply intent that, irrespective of their nature, those documents are in strict compliance with the credit terms. This limited concern is well expressed in footnote D on the form in the disclaimer of any responsibility for ' . . . validity, sufficiency, genuineness or accuracy of the shipping, insurance or any other documents . . .'.

A final indication of the practices of banks, based on their vulnerability as principals in the documentary credit contracts, appears in footnote A which gives the opening bank rights over the documents, goods and proceeds of sale thereof in respect of outstanding liabilities.

The discussions with a buyer on the category of credit required and the documentation to be provided are often included in negotiating the order or contract, and direct contact is through an exporter's export sale executive who is not necessarily a financial expert. To assist in these circumstances the Simplification of International Trade Procedures Board (SITPRO), 29 Glasshouse Street, London, W1R 5RG, has produced an excellent guide for export sales executives which is both convenient to carry (pocket book size) and comprehensive in content. It covers concisely the points to be discussed within the exporting company prior to visiting the customer and those which should be agreed during the negotiations in order that the credit is in terms acceptable to both parties.

Types of documentary credit

Within the three main categories of credit there are the following types meeting individual needs.

The transferable credit

Many exporters buy in raw materials or components which may represent a high percentage of the value of the end products. Others may act solely as middlemen whose knowledge of overseas markets or of a particular range of products enables them to buy from manufacturers and sell to foreign buyers to the mutual benefit of all concerned. Often the expertise of these middlemen is their principal asset and they neither have, nor indeed require, a substantial capital base. Therein however lies a problem. The manufacturer or supplier of components or raw materials may not be prepared to sell to the exporter unless there is a security of payment similar to that enjoyed by the exporter under an irrevocable (or an irrevocable and confirmed) letter of credit.

To meet this situation a transferable credit may be issued. Under the terms of such credits the beneficiary has the right to request the advising bank to make the credit available in whole or part to one or more other parties and, although the bank is under no obligation to do so, it would not normally refuse upon payment of transfer charges. A transferable credit may be transferred once only although this may be to two or more 'second' beneficiaries and the transfer is on identical terms and conditions specified in the original credit with the following exceptions:

1 The amount may be reduced as may any unit prices shown.
2 The expiry date, the latest date for shipment and the last date for presentation of documents (within the validity) may all be reduced or curtailed.
3 The percentage for which insurance cover must be effected may be increased in order to provide the amount of cover required under the original credit.
4 The name of the first beneficiary can be substituted for that of the applicant (opener) for the original credit but if the applicant's name is required by the original credit to appear in any document other than the invoice, this requirement will apply also in the transferred credit.

The substitution of name provision is vital to a transferable credit and care should be taken that no document other than the invoice requires the applicant's name to be disclosed under the terms of the original credit. If this is not achieved then the second beneficiary may be able to contact the applicant for the original credit soliciting further business and effectively cut out the first beneficiary. It is precisely to prevent this danger that the first beneficiary has the right under a transferable credit to substitute his invoices for those of the second beneficiary and to claim the difference (his profit) under the original credit.

Back-to-back credit

(act solely, knowledge of overseas markets)

An alternative method of approaching the problem of the middlemen as detailed under transferable credits is the back-to-back credit but, it must be stressed, many banks in the United Kingdom and abroad are reluctant to open this type of credit. Basically the middleman approaches his bank with the credit in his favour requesting that it be accepted as security for a credit to be issued in favour of the supplier in similar terms but for a reduced amount and validity. The effect on the supplier is similar to receiving a transferred credit, but the bank opening a back-to-back credit has a liability for which it must look to the middleman who, as we have remarked earlier, may have expertise but little asset backing.

If the documents presented under a back-to-back credit are identical to those required under the original credit with the obvious exception of invoices, then in theory the bank should have no problem but in practice difficulties can and have occurred. Banks prefer the transferable credit solution which involves the advising or confirming bank in no greater liability than was accepted under the original credit.

Revolving credits

A revolving credit is one which according to its terms may be renewed or reinstated in amount without the opener being required to request an amendment to enable this to be effected.

There are two methods by which this can be achieved: the credit may revolve in relation to time or value. Where time is the governing factor the credit might be opened with a validity of twelve months with the provision that £10,000 per month is available during that time irrespective of whether any drawing took place during the preceding month. The credit could be either non-cumulative or cumulative. If the former any sum not drawn in a given month is automatically cancelled and may not be utilized in the succeeding month. Conversely if the credit is cumulative sums not drawn during a particular month may be carried over to the succeeding month. Where value revolves the credit is re-instated after documents have been presented **or** when they have been received by the opening bank, according to the instructions given.

Both varieties of revolving credit will appeal to exporters and buyers who have a constant stream of business and wish to avoid repetitive arrangements for opening or amending letters of credit. Bankers and openers are likely to prefer credits revolving in relation to time as they have a quantifiable liability figure whereas credits revolving in relation to value have an incalculable liability unless the wording includes an overall amount payable under the credit. If this is included and the credit also provides that reinstatement can only take place when the opening bank has authorized the advising bank to do so (this being when the opener has paid for the documents), the credit may be a useful way of phasing deliveries if the total value of the contract is high in relation to the buyer's credit standing.

Red clause credits

In certain types of trading the exporter will purchase goods or commodities from a number of suppliers in order to make up the total quantity required by the buyer. An example is the wool trade where shippers may purchase from farmers over a wide area and the initial outlay can be considerable and may outstand for a significant period. To facilitate the supplier's purchases the buyer may arrange a letter of credit which permits the advising or confirming bank to make an advance before presentation of documents which is repaid through a deduction from th ment ultimately made against those documents. In the event of those documents not being presented the bank which has made the advance is entitled to claim reimbursement from the issuing bank. The intriguing title of this type of credit derives from the fact that the clause allowing the advance was traditionally written in red ink to stress its importance; this practice is no longer followed.

A similar purpose to that served by the red clause credit is achieved by inserting in a documentary credit the provision that a stated amount or percentage may be drawn down in advance of the receipt of documents against presentation of a banker's guarantee that it will be refunded in the event of failure to produce documents conforming to the terms and conditions of the credit prior to expiry.

Letters of credit covering payment for services

For convenience we will regard letters of credit opened in order to pay for services as a separate type although they differ very little in principle from credits covering payment for goods. The requirements regarding amounts, revocability, confirmation and expiry are identical but clearly the documentary stipulations differ since there is no movement of goods. The credit will normally call for invoices indicating the service in question and confirmation that it has been provided. On occasion a document from the recipient (the opener) confirming it has received the service may be called for; this is not considered normal documentary credit practice because it means the opener can effectively render the credit useless by withholding the required confirmation.

If circumstances permit, an ideal solution is a confirmation from a third party acceptable to both the supplier and the recipient of the service; this will provide an element of security to both parties. It is also not unusual for a credit of this type to provide for a number of payments against appropriate documentation covering stages in the provision of a service extending over a period of time. This can act as a builder of confidence between the parties which can be more difficult with a single payment.

Standby credits

This is a generic term covering credits which are differentiated from others in that the parties do not expect them to be used unless an emergency or irregularity occurs. For example exporter and buyer might agree to trade on open account terms but with a standby credit payable solely against the beneficiary's signed declaration that the buyer had failed to make payment for a delivery stating the date, particulars and carrying vessel involved.

Another context in which standby credits are used is as a substitute for banker's guarantees which we shall be considering in a later chapter. In some countries commercial banks are precluded from issuing guarantees, a function which is reserved to fidelity companies. In these circumstances the bank may issue a credit in favour of a buyer payable against its certificate that the contractor has failed to perform the terms of the contract which, we shall observe, has a similar effect to an on-demand guarantee. Again the parties do not anticipate the credit being used if performance of the contract is carried out; it exists only as a standby precaution.

Documentary Credits as the Exporter Sees Them

The wording on documentary credits varies considerably according to the issuing bank and country, practice in the advising bank and country and the individual sale and purchase of goods which underlie the credit. There is no internationally accepted rigid format although the order in which items appear, the orderer, amount, expiry and documentation are usually very similar. Exhibits 7.2, 7.3 and 7.4 depict a collection of relatively common documentary credit wordings but there are multiple variations. To assist in familiarizing the reader with credits I have chosen as examples three which are conveyed by the United Kingdom advising or confirming banks, to exporters, on their own paper and which have not been 'economical in words'.

One of the disadvantages of modern high speed communication methods, much as they are appreciated by international traders, is that the instructions are received in a very abbreviated form and are often conveyed to the beneficiary exactly as received. However, with care, these can be translated into a form similar to that in the specimens. Exporters will also frequently receive documentary credits on the paper of the issuing bank with a covering letter from the advising or confirming bank specifying what engagement, if any, they accept including confirmation where appropriate and adding any clarification of the credit they consider necessary.

Exhibit 7.2: Specimen Documentary Credit

WEST BARMID BANK PLC   International Branch
                                         P O Box 99
                                         Main Street
                                         County Town

                                         19th December 1993

PDB Exports (93) Ltd
222 Arcade Square
UK Town

Dears Sirs

Documentary Credit No 567/3/289 M

We have been advised by the Friendly Individuals Bank, Happytown, Anywhere that they have opened an irrevocable Documentary Credit Number 567/3/289 M in your favour for £25,000 (say) Twenty Five Thousand Pounds Sterling for account of Excited Importers Incorporated.

This credit is to be available by draft(s) drawn at sight for 100% CIF Invoice Value on the Friendly Individuals Bank,

Happytown, Anywhere clearly marked that it is/they are 'drawn under Credit No 567/3/289 M' and accompanied by the undermentioned documents:

Invoices in triplicate indicating the goods are of UK origin.

Packing List in triplicate.

Inspection Certificate signed and dated at the port of shipment issued by the Reliable Inspection Co. Ltd.

Insurance Policy or Certificate in duplicate covering Institute Cargo Clauses (A) and War and Strikes as per the appropriate Institute Clauses, for the CIF Invoice Value plus 10%.

Complete set clean 'on board' ocean bills of lading issued to order, black endorsed marked 'freight paid' and 'notify Excited Importers Incorporated'.

Covering the shipment of:

30 Silver Plated Dragon Vases as Proforma Invoice No 7254 dated 15.10.93 Price CIF Happytown.

From Southampton to Happytown Port not later than 15th January 1994 Part Shipments not allowed Transshipment allowed.

The credit is available for presentation until 15th February 1994 in the United Kingdom.

We reserve the right to make a charge not exceeding £50 for additional costs arising should documents be presented which do not comply with the terms of this credit.

Friendly Individuals Bank advise us that this credit is irrevocable on their part. This letter is solely an advice of the credit established by the bank and conveys no engagement on our part.

Except so far as otherwise expressly stated, this credit is subject
to Uniform Customs and Practice for Documentary Credits 1993
Revision International Chamber of Commerce Publication
No 500.

Yours faithfully

A. Manager
West Barmid Bank Plc

Exhibit 7.3: Specimen Documentary Credit

WEST BARMID BANK PLC   International Branch
                                    P O Box 99
                                    Main Street
                                    County Town

                                    14th January 1994

PDB Exports (93) Ltd
222 Arcade Square
UK Town

Dears Sirs

Documentary Credit No 567/3/290 M

We shall be obliged if you will kindly note that the State Bank
of Ruritania, Capital City, Ruritania have opened an irrevocable
Documentary Credit in your favour in accordance with the
details given below.

For Account of: State Ministry of Finance

Amount: £50,000 (Fifty Thousand Pounds Sterling)
Expiry Date: 15th July 1994 in the United Kingdom

This credit is to be made available by draft(s) at 90 days after sight on the West Barmid Bank PLC, International Branch, PO Box 99, Main Street, Countytown clearly marked that it is/they are 'drawn under State Bank of Ruritania Documentary Credit No 568/3/290 M' and accompanied by documents as stipulated below.

Draft(s) is/are to be drawn to the extent of 100% of the full invoice value.

Documents required

Invoice in triplicate certifying goods are in accordance with Proforma Invoice No 6482/93.

Certificate of UK origin issued by a Chamber of Commerce and countersigned by the Ruritanian Consulate.

Air Consignment Note (Airway Bill) indicating goods consigned to the Ruritanian State Ministry of Finance Capital City marked 'Freight Paid'.

Covering: 10,000 Numbered Lambs Identification Jackets for cold weather use.

Price £5 each CPT Capital City Airport. Despatch from Heathrow Airport UK. Part shipments allowed Transshipment prohibited.

We reserve the right to make a charge for any costs which arise should documents presented not comply with the credit terms.

This credit irrevocable on the part of the State Bank of Ruritania, Capital City, Ruritania is also confirmed by the West Barmid Bank Plc in accordance with the terms of the undertaking expressed in Article 9b of the Uniform Customs and Practice for Documentary Credits, ICC Publication No 500.

Except in so far as otherwise expressly stated, this credit is subject to Uniform Customs and Practice for Documentary Credits 1993 Revision International Chamber of Commerce Publication No 500.

Yours faithfully

A. Manager
West Barmid Bank Plc

Exhibit 7.4: Specimen Documentary Credit

WEST BARMID BANK PLC   International Branch
                                              P O Box 99
                                              Main Street
                                              County Town

                                              21st January 1994

PDB Exports (93) Ltd
222 Arcade Square
UK Town

Dears Sirs

Documentary Credit No 687/2/340 L

We have been advised by the Shangri La Banking Corporation, Utopia City, Anywhere that they have opened an irrevocable Documentary Credit No 687/2/340 L in your favour the particulars of which are as follows:

Opener: Tranquil Importers Unlimited
Amount: US $60,000 (Sixty Thousand US Dollars)
Expiry Date: 8th July 1994 in the United Kingdom

This credit is available by drafts at sight on the Shangri La Banking Corporation, Utopia City, Anywhere in the currency of the credit indicating they are drawn under that bank's Documentary Credit No 687/2/340 L. Drafts are to be drawn for the full CIF Invoice Value and must be accompanied by the following documents:

Invoices in quadruplicate indicating import licence reference UR 411 and bearing your signed certificate that the goods shipped as per Proforma Invoice No 76-20-14 dated 1st December 1993. Your certificate that one negotiable copy of the Bill of Lading has been sent direct to Tranquil Importers Unlimited by express, registered airmail.

Insurance Policy or Certificate in duplicate in the same currency as the credit for the invoice value plus 15% covering Institute Cargo Clauses (A), Institute War and Strikes Riots and Civil Commotions Clauses.

2/3 Ocean Bills of Lading made out to order, blank endorsed, marked 'Freight Paid' dated not later than 25th June 1994.

Covering a shipment of:

6,000 assorted volumes of 'Beautiful Thoughts' reading manuals at $10 per volume CIF Utopia City. Partial Shipment not allowed Transshipment allowed

We reserve the right to make a charge for any costs which arise should documents presented not comply with the Credit Terms.

Shangri La Banking Corporation, Utopia City, Anywhere advise us that this credit is irrevocable on their part. This letter is solely an advice of the credit established by that bank and conveys no engagement on our part.

160

Except so far as otherwise expressly stated, this credit is subject to Uniform Customs and Practice for Documentary Credits 1993 Revision International Chamber of Commerce Publication No 500.

Yours faithfully

A. Manager
West Barmid Bank Plc

Exhibit 7.2 is a documentary credit irrevocable by the opening bank, but not confirmed, in sterling with drafts drawn at sight covering a shipment by sea. Exhibit 7.3 is again an irrevocable unconfirmed credit in sterling but with drafts drawn at 90 days sight covering a consignment by air. Exhibit 7.4 is an irrevocable confirmed documentary credit in United States Dollars covering a shipment by sea where one negotiable copy of the bill of lading has been forwarded by the ship's bag to avoid the possibility of demurrage should the shipment arrive before the documents.

Each of the specimens is representative of many hundreds of documentary credits passing through the banking system. Readers should familiarize themselves with the general format before we turn to the many individual considerations which may concern a particular exporter and the implications of United Customs and Practice for Documentary Credits which you will have noticed is referred to in all three specimens.

8

Documentary Credits: Securing Payment

You may recall that the quotation was described as a milestone in securing a successful sale. Once the quotation is given, the basis for the transaction is firm unless the buyer rejects the quotation. A similar milestone is reached in securing payment when the exporter receives a documentary credit though the advising bank. Up to that point the manufacture of the goods may not have begun and if it has, the goods will not have entered the final build up towards shipment. Once the documentary credit has been accepted as in conformity with the exporter's needs, clearance is given to those responsible for the shipment preparations.

In these circumstances it is difficult to understand why, each year, a large number of exporters – after receiving their documentary credits and checking the shipment or validity date and observing it to be three or six months hence – place the document in a drawer for perusal nearer the time. Perhaps it is the pressure of current work; the shipment due out next week seems so much more urgent and demands last minute checking; or perhaps it is a degree of complacency; the exporter has faithfully followed all the advice given earlier in this book and the result must be a happy conclusion. Whatever the reason, had the exporter seen the number of instances experienced by the writer when customers have unearthed the credit a few weeks or even days before shipment, only to discover to their horror that the terms cannot be fulfilled, they would have given immediate attention to checking the contents of every credit on the day it was received or as soon after as possible. If mistakes have occurred there is then the time available to seek an amendment or discuss the problem whereas a mistake discovered at the eleventh hour is often beyond correction.

The variations in methods of sale and complexity between any two exports mean that the areas within the terms of a documentary credit which may be particularly sensitive to mistakes will similarly vary. Some of the most common causes for concern will now be examined. In doing so we are assisted yet again by the International Chamber of Commerce which, with the assistance of the financial and international business communities, has compiled and published a set of rules of practice on documentary credit procedures which seeks to achieve standard interpretations and to clarify, for the benefit of all parties, what has now become internationally acceptable practice. Publication No 500 is entitled *Uniform Customs and Practice for Documentary Credits 500* and is obtainable from the same offices of the International Chamber as shown in chapter 6 when discussing their *Uniform Rules for Collection.*

I know that many colleagues with whom I have worked through the years will agree that *Uniform Customs* is a booklet not just for bankers. With its aid,exporters and buyers alike are better equipped to understand documentary credits and the decisions which banks make on presentation of documents. Banks would certainly welcome a greater spread of knowledge as the misunderstandings and friction in bank-customer relations from rejections of documents presented are a constant source of concern. The booklet, which is essential reading for examination students, is also therefore recommended to all readers together with *UCP 500 and 400 Compared* (publication No 511) where exporters can learn of the changes which have taken place since the previous revision, which was in force up to the 31st December 1993.

Examination of a Credit on Receipt

A suggested pattern for examination follows but exporters would be wise to add or amend according to individual circumstances. References to uniform customs and practice for documentary credits will use the abbreviation UCP and it must be remembered that UCP articles frequently contain the qualification 'unless otherwise stipulated in the credit' thus providing freedom to override. The following are the questions usually asked:

Is the credit subject to UCP? Most credits are and will bear an annotation to that effect probably as a final or penultimate paragraph.

Is the category of credit (such as confirmed irrevocable, irrevocable or revocable) in accordance with your requirements for security as advised to your buyer? Remember if no indication is given the credit is regarded as irrevocable (unless it is a credit issued previously subject to UCP 400 when, in the absence of any indication to the contrary, it is regarded as revocable) but a **confirmed** irrevocable credit must specifically state that it bears the confirmation of the bank advising it to the beneficiary.

Do the terms for payment (sight of usance) agree with those included in your quotation to the buyer? The number of days after sight in a usance bill should correspond to the credit you have allowed your buyer.

Is the credit payable in the United Kingdom or abroad? If it is only payable abroad there may be delay unless the advising bank is prepared to negotiate; check the position.

Are the names and addresses of both the buyer and yourselves correct? Apart from affecting your ability to comply with the credit terms a mistake in this area can have other serious implications. The bank might query as the 'rightful' beneficiary a Smith and Company whose invoice showed a different address, or a cheque issued in payment in favour of 'Smyth and Company' might not be acceptable for the account of Smith and Company.

Is the amount of the credit correct? It is easy for a buyer unintentionally to overlook its responsibility for incidental charges as agreed with the exporter and to issue the credit covering only the basic price of the goods.

Do the validity and latest shipment dates (if included) provide adequate time for the formalities necessary in the preparation of documents and, of course, the production of goods. Common pitfalls include infrequent scheduled sailings to the stipulated destination which may defeat efforts to conform to the latest shipment date, or an underestimation of the time necessary to obtain countersignature of a certification of origin by a consulate or specialized chamber of commerce. Remember also that, in general, reliance on third parties in providing documentation required under a credit, while unavoidable, always involves a risk of delay. It is preferable to have a little leeway in the validity and latest shipment dates and not an overtight timetable.

Watch for any requirement that a particular shipping company or insurer must be used as this can create considerable administrative as well as time problems.

In studying the documentary requirements set out in the credit, check that they conform with those you have agreed with the buyer both as regards individual documents and the list as a whole. Sometimes a buyer seeks to remedy a lapse of memory by slipping in an additional document. The expense and inconvenience to you in supplying the extra document may well call for immediate discussion with the buyer.

Documents covering transport of goods are a fertile area for misunderstanding. Some of the problems may be foreseen and avoided if, upon receipt, the requirements of the credit regarding transport documents are given particular attention with the aid of *Uniform Customs and Practice*. The following are among the questions most usefully asked.

Is the transport document called for appropriate to the mode(s) of transport agreed with the buyer (air, rail, sea, water, road or post)? An obvious question? Maybe, but it is not unknown for buyers to decide between initial negotiations and the opening of the credit that there is a higher degree of urgency than was envisaged or for there to have been a genuine misunderstanding as to how the goods were to be dispatched.

If transport is to be by sea, does the credit reflect the agreement reached with the buyer as to the type of document to be accepted? Unlike transport by air, road, rail or inland waterway where a standard form of transport document appropriate to the mode is usual, and by courier or post where a post receipt or certification of posting or a document indicating collection for dispatch by a courier service is expected, sea transport can be evidenced by a variety of documents. Uniform Customs and

Practice is essential in understanding the information which is required to appear in each type, but one or two principles are worthy of emphasis at this point. Bills of lading are of several types. Marine or ocean bills of lading are documents of title normally issued in sets of two or three negotiable copies (although sole bills are not uncommon) and will be required to indicate that goods have actually been shipped on board the carrying vessel as distinct from having been received for shipment. Charter party bills of lading arise where an exporter has chartered a vessel to carry its cargo exclusively and are particularly common where bulk shipments are concerned such as commodities and oil. Such bills are not acceptable by banks as complying with letters of credit unless the credit specifically calls for or permits charter party bills.

A sea waybill is non-negotiable and is often used where the voyage time is short and involves the danger of the goods arriving before documents have been passed through the banking system. As mentioned in chapter 6 this can have serious repercussions in the form of high demurrage charges. Again sea waybills are only acceptable presentation under a credit which specifically requires them to be tendered. The practice of issuing multimodal transport documents is also recognized in documentary credit provisions and a credit may call for a transport document covering two or more different modes of transport. These and many other invaluable indications as to the acceptability of transport documents under letters of credit appear in *UCP 500*, and the International Chamber of Commerce have, in the writer's opinion, improved considerably the method of setting out requirements in comparison with the last revision, *UCP 400*, in addition to the inclusion of material relating to techniques introduced into transport documentation since that time.

Will the transport document I receive be issued by a Freight Forwarder? If the answer is yes, the credit should indicate such a document to be acceptable presentation unless the forwarder is shown as a multimodal transport operator or carrier and has signed in that capacity, or has signed as a named agent for the named carrier or multimodal transport operator in which cases the bank will accept the document under the Uniform Customs and Practice.

Am I shipping goods which are in a hazardous category and which, in consequence, will be carried on the deck of the vessel? If the answer is affirmative the credit should be examined to ensure that a specific authorization is included for the goods to be loaded on deck. Should the credit not include such a provision bills of lading indicating deck shipment will be refused. It is also important in this context of claused bills of lading to add that any clause appearing which declares either the goods or the packaging to be defective will cause the bank to refuse acceptance unless the credit indicates that a particular clause or notation is permissible.

Ascertain if the credit calls for an insurance document, whether a policy or a certificate is required. Decide if you can comply and if the risks to be covered are acceptable within the terms of your agreement with the buyer.

Consider in detail each of the other documents required – are they strictly according to what was agreed? For example, who is to issue the certificate of origin? Is it to be countersigned? What origin (or origins) are permissible?

If you are intending to effect part shipments satisfy yourself that the credit does not preclude this course.

Is there a port specified from which the shipment is to take place and one which is to be the destination or are you given an option? If ports are nominated this is mandatory under the credit and documents showing other options will be rejected. Check therefore that the nominations are correct.

Is the description of the goods (which we have agreed earlier should be concise) both correct and in keeping with the contract of sale? A generic description, preferably with a mention of any proforma invoice, is ideal provided it does not conflict with the contract and enables identification of the goods.

When you have completed your examination make sure that if you are using a forwarding agent, the agency is provided with a copy in order that any problems which it may see are brought to your attention. One final point – it would be well worth considering obtaining copies of check lists published by the Simplification of International Trade Procedures Board (SITPRO) (address as in chapter 7), particularly if the task of checking the credit is to be undertaken by staff who are not fully experienced.

Amending Letters of Credit

Unless an exporter, after receiving a credit which differs from its understanding of the agreement with the buyer, is prepared to revise the intended procedure to enable compliance with the terms, it will have to seek an appropriate amendment. This can be done through the advising bank or direct to the buyer; personally I prefer the latter as it should be quicker and, of course, only the buyer can authorize the amendment. There might be some merit in keeping the advising bank aware of your request to the buyer marked 'for information only'. Amendments are subject to a commission charge by the banks and, in respect of irrevocable credits, must be agreed by all parties.

The Doctrine of Strict Compliance

This is the term applied to the acceptability of documents presented under credits and the importance of the word 'strict' cannot be overemphasized. We have already noted that a letter of credit is a conditional undertaking by a bank; the doctrine makes clear that the conditions must be met.

Before considering the examination which every exporter should make of every set of documents to be presented under a credit to endeavour to ensure strict compliance, shall we refute one widely held misapprehension, namely that an exporter who is a customer of the advising or negotiating bank is entitled to special consideration on presenting documents due to that relationship. It was suggested in chapter 7 that there are advantages in requesting a buyer to ask its bank to arrange for the credit to be routed through the exporter's bank, either as advising or confirming bank according to the category of credit. This is so and if it can be achieved (the decision lies in the hands of the issuing bank) the beneficiary (exporter) is able to discuss any problems arising with management and staff which must be helpful. It is also possible, as we shall observe later, that the relationship may assist in discovering ways in which payment can be made against documents showing minor discrepancies. What is not possible, as many exporters wrongly imagine, is that the

169

bank will be less diligent in its examination of documents, or even overlook a discrepancy because it is dealing with a beneficiary which is also a customer. Why is this so?

The answer is that in the context of a documentary credit the customer relationship is immaterial and in fact does not exist in relation to the credit. The advising or confirming bank is the agent of its principal, the issuing bank, and in that capacity has a duty to ensure documents are in strict compliance with the credit. Of course it also has responsibilities to the beneficiary (under UCP) as a party to the credit but these apply equally irrespective of whether or not that beneficiary banks with the advising or confirming bank. For further information on the legal aspects readers should refer to the companion volume in this series, *Principles of Law Relating to Overseas Trade*, as the above explanation is intended only to refer to the normal facets of banking practice.

It is also pertinent that there is considerable case law on the subject of strict compliance and banks are not unmindful of this in their scrupulous examination of documents. If the advising bank pays against documents which are subsequently rejected by the issuing bank due to discrepancies, there is no defence on the grounds that the discrepancy was so minor as to be without significance; the bank is not expected to be the arbitrator and acts as such at its peril, risking incurring an irrecoverable loss.

Discrepancies in Presentations

It is a sad fact, confirmed by regular analyses, that well over 50 per cent of first presentations of documents to banks in the United Kingdom under documentary letters of credit are rejected due to discrepancies. Even more distressing, despite constant publicity for the figures there appears to be little improvement and the problem is not confined to the United Kingdom. The implications are widely felt. Exporters would surely be shocked in these days of cost consciousness if they were to calculate the interest lost or paid on delayed settlements according to whether their accounts were in debit or credit. Banks likewise suffer loss in the event of re-presentations having to be processed and, as will be seen in the specimen credits, they now reserve the right to make a charge in these circumstances. The goods themselves may arrive and incur demurrage while methods of dealing with the situation are being considered. Last, but most important of all, if the discrepancies cannot be rectified and the documents re-presented within the validity of the credit, the exporter may have to resort to other methods of seeking payment for the goods, thus forfeiting the hard won security provided by the credit.

Experience shows that a small but significant proportion of discrepancies would have been avoidable if the initial exam-ination of the credit terms, on its receipt, had been as thorough as recommended earlier. A substantial number of discrepancies are due to a lack of attention in the pre-preparation check which should always take place, and a failure to appreciate or interpret the conditions of the credit; these will be looked at more closely later in this chapter. Finally discrepancies obviously can and do occur; they are due to circumstances beyond the control of the exporter but one must comment that these are a relatively small minority.

The Pre-presentation Examination

This will ideally consist of three separate operations, and all should be conducted but the order in which they take place is optional. They are as follows.

Check the documents against each other to ensure they are compatible in their description of the goods; although only the invoice need match exactly that in the credit the remaining documents must show a description not incompatible with that in the credit. Your check should also cover weights, shipping marks, packaging and other details which must not vary between the documents on which they appear.

Examine each document individually to ensure that it is prop-erly completed, dated and signed where necessary. Particularly pay attention to the less obvious omissions, for example certifi-cates of origin signed but without the authenticating stamp of a chamber of commerce.

With the letter of credit before you, compare each document

called for with that which you are intending to present. Some of the most common discrepancies found in documents presented are described below.

We will assume at this stage that the examination of the credit terms at the time of receipt, which was stressed as vitally important earlier, has been carried out conscientiously and that documents which have been **prepared by the exporter** are therefore in strict compliance. In respect of those documents only particulars which will have been added after shipment will be mentioned. In the order in which requirements under a credit are normally listed (see exhibits 7.2-7.4 inclusive) the first stipulation concerned in this final check is the credit amount.

Ensure that no last minute variance in the quantity of goods shipped has either breached the credit provisions on quantity or caused the invoice amount to exceed that of the credit, allowing for any tolerance permitted by such words as 'about' or 'approximately'. In case preparation of the bill of exchange has taken place at this stage (rather than before shipment to be dated later), is it properly drawn up in accordance with the advice offered in chapter 6 and are details as per the credit? The most common mistakes are bills drawn on the wrong party (for instance, on the buyer and not on the bank), where the credit stipulates the latter, and an omission of the required reference to the letter of credit in question.

Invoices are on occasions presented describing the goods in a manner which the exporter would contend is 'commonplace within the trade and identical to the description appearing in the credit', but is not word for word. An example might be apricot jam or apricot conserve or apricot preserve, all descriptions which appear very similar to the layman but might have significant technical differences to the expert or within the trade. Such a presentation is unacceptable. It is not just that bankers are but common folk unfamiliar with the jargon of customers' trade; true though this may be, the reason is again that the description is not in strict compliance with the credit and bankers, even if they were competent to do so, are precluded from accepting it. This is equally true with a differing description which might seem from a common sense standpoint to be the same requirement in the goods, for example a credit calling for 'used trucks' and an invoice covering 'secondhand trucks'.

The transport document is probably the most vulnerable where discrepancies are concerned. On receipt check that it is in compliance with the credit by conforming to all the requirements we noted when making the initial check when the credit was first received; in all probability your forwarding agent, if used, will have monitored these but time taken in confirming accuracy is never wasted. Ensure that no clauses which indicate a defective condition of the goods and/or the packaging have been superimposed during the loading of the goods, that it is an on board bill of lading if the credit specifies this, and that you have a full set. If the bill is to order do not forget to endorse it in blank before presentation. Verify that the ports of shipment and destination do not conflict with the credit, and that the transport document is marked 'freight paid' or 'freight payable at destination' as required. Avoid the pitfall of presenting a document marked 'freight to be prepaid' in lieu of the former; there must be evidence that the carrier has **received** payment.

Is the date of shipment within any time limits expressed in the credit? In considering the credit requirements regarding transshipment remember that we are not concerned with the small print provisions in a bill of lading which give the captain the right in an emergency involving the safety of the vessel or crew to transship (there is also a similar right to ship on deck or jettison in case of emergency). If the credit precludes transshipment and the Uniform Custom and Practice does not indicate that the circumstances are such that the transport document required is one which can be accepted showing transhipment notwithstanding that prohibition, the bill of lading, to be acceptable, must show no intention to transship in the normal course of the journey.

Insurance documents are also prone to discrepancies, the most common probably being a failure to endorse where necessary and in the risks covered being different to those specified in the credit. Less frequent but still significant are cases where the requirements of minimum cover for the invoice value plus 10 per cent has not been met, insurance is not in the same currency as the credit and the presentation of an insurance document bearing a later date than appears as the issue date on the transport document. Unless specifically authorized in the credit, cover notes issued by brokers are not acceptable in lieu of insurance policies or certificates.

Finally note any latest shipment date and the expiry date of the credit by which documents must be presented in order to the bank if payment is to be made. If you have in your initial examination of the credit verified that the expiry date allows sufficient time there should be no problem, but it is still wise to present as early as possible in case the bank should return documents for discrepancies. This may give you the vital extra time to make such amendments as are practical and still represent before expiry.

In the case of credits expiring on a day upon which the bank to whom presentation is to be made is normally closed the expiry date is extended to the first following business day on which the bank is open. This provision applies also to the period of time, after the date upon which transport documents are issued, during which they may be presented. Although credits will sometimes stipulate the latest time for presentation, which must not be later than the expiry date of the credit, it is more usual for no mention to be made in which case the requirements of not later than 21 days after issuance will apply.

In calculating the period in relation to your particular transport document remember what constitutes the date of issue. For air carriage the date will be that upon which the airway bill is issued or, if a flight date was required to be shown by the credit, that date. Bills of lading evidencing on board loading are deemed to have as the date of issue that on which the bill is issued or, if an on board annotation appears, the date appearing therein. In the case of documents covering other than carriage by air and evidencing that the goods have been either dis-patched or received for irrevocable dispatch the date on the document or on any endorsement indicating receipt, whichever is the later, shall apply.

Occasionally a credit will be received which adds to the normal latest shipment date, a qualification of 'on or about' which the bank will interpret under Uniform Custom and Practice as allow-ing shipment up to and including five days before the stipulated date or up to and including five days thereafter. Similarly UCP provides useful clarification should the shipment requirement read during the 'first half', 'second half', 'beginning', 'middle' or 'end' of a month and banks will interpret these descriptions accordingly. However exporters would be well advised to avoid such terminology in their agreements with buyers as they do introduce a possibility of misunderstanding which is eliminated by the inclusion of a specific date.

The Simplification of Trade Procedures Organisation also has available a useful check list, including many of the above points, for use by staff preparing documents for presentation. A small but important practical detail is that the list is independent of any other literature and ideally suited for ready reference.

Action in the Event of Discrepancies

Despite following all the advice given in this book, discrepancies can and will occur in presentations under documentary credits. If they do and the bank returns the documents what action can the exporter take? Speed is essential. If the discrepancies are capable of amendment by the exporter – for example omissions of signature, authentications, and dates, or misspelt or incomplete descriptions – this should be done immediately. Where errors or omissions are those of others, urgent steps should be taken to endeavour to have the relevant documents corrected. In both cases, provided amendments can be made enabling re-presentation within the time limit imposed by the credit or UCP, payment may be made and the security represented by the documentary credit is not lost. Where this is not possible the exporter has several options, but all will impair the security in so far as the buyer's consent is necessary and the exporter no longer looks only to the bank for payment.

A request may be made to the buyer for an amendment to the credit terms to enable the documents to be acceptable as presented notwithstanding the discrepancy(ies). Examples of discrepancies which might be dealt with in this way are claused bills of lading, whereas errors and omissions on documents which would be necessary to achieve customs clearance, such as certificates of origin, must be remedied.

If amendments necessary are time consuming and render it uncertain whether re-presentation can be achieved within the existing expiry date it may be possible to persuade the buyer to authorize a short extension, but care must be taken to minimize the risk of the goods arriving before the documents with the consequent danger of demurrage charges.

If the discrepancies are considered minor, in the opinion of the bank, they may be prepared to pay on presentation either 'under reserve' or 'with recourse' to the exporter. This indicates an informal agreement that should documents be rejected by the issuing bank due to the discrepancies in question this exporter will repay the sum received. Because the agreement is informal the offer of payment on this basis is normally made by a bank only to a beneficiary which is also a customer or to one which is very well known to them, and this is a further reason for an exporter endeavouring to have documentary credits routed through its own bank.

Provided the discrepancies are not of such a nature that the paying or negotiating bank is reasonably certain that the issuing bank will **not** make payment against the documents, the exporter may be able to receive payment against its indemnity or that of its bank. The indemnity will undertake to refund the payment should the documents be rejected by the issuing bank due to the discrepancies and is, in effect, a formalization of the procedure in paying 'under reserve' or 'with recourse'. Although any indemnity is initially for the benefit of the bank(s), the buyer may on occasion request that it be extended as a condition of authorizing payment by the issuing bank. A word of warning to the exporter who is asked to provide a banker's indemnity: it is a real liability and should be regarded as such both in respect of the amount of the company's assets which it effectively attaches over its duration and the need to pursue its release actively.

The documents may be sent by the advising bank to the issuing bank under cover of the credit but on a collection basis. The effect is to revert to the conditions and procedures for a documentary collection as described in chapter 6.

It will thus be seen that the documentary credit provides both a speedy and secure method of payment provided the necessary precautions are taken to minimize the risk of discrepancies, but that a lapse of memory or worse, a lack of care and attention, can return the exporter to the reliance on his buyer alone, destroying the entire framework upon which the method is based.

9

Banker's Guarantees (Bonds) and Indemnities

In considering documentary credits, it has been apparent that in assessing degrees of risk there comes a point when a seller requires the undertaking of a bank in preference to that of the buyer, but this is not the only instance where a banker's promise is called for in support of a contractual obligation between seller and buyer. In this chapter we look at a number of situations requiring bankers' commitments. The first group, contract guarantees, is at the instigation of a buyer, not a seller.

Many potential buyers ordering goods or whole projects of great value will adopt the method of inviting tenders using competitive quotations from sellers worldwide. The advantages are immediately apparent: the chances of any suppliers being unaware of the opportunity are minimized and the competition engendered should ensure that prices are keen. Disadvantages lie in the danger of some tenderers withdrawing before the date on which tenders are considered, the adjudication date, or refusing to sign any contract awarded. The risk may seem small, but the appearance of unforeseen business between tender closure and adjudication can threaten capacity to supply or some tenderers might quite simply fall victim to over-confidence, realizing on award that they are unable to accept the order. For the buyer the results can be both expensive and embarrassing in view of the size of the business. If the tenderer refuses to sign a contract the buyer must either offer the award to an alternative tenderer or may feel obliged to re-issue the invitation.

Traditionally the problem has been overcome by tenderers being required to accompany their bids with a cash deposit which served as an indication that they were serious in their intentions to supply if successful. This was however both inconvenient and expensive for the large majority of perfectly genuine tenderers and, in consequence, it became common to accept in lieu of cash a banker's guarantee or bond (the terms are, in this context, interchangeable). The guarantor undertook to pay the sum, usually specified by the buyer as being between two and five per cent of the tender amount, in the event of the tenderer either withdrawing before adjudication or refusing to sign any contract awarded.

Because tender guarantees replace the traditional cash deposit, they are normally expected to provide the same degree of protection to the buyer. As this was the ability to retain the cash already deposited without the tenderer being able to take any preventative action, a banker's tender guarantee is almost invariably payable upon the first demand of the beneficiary **without contestation**.

An example of how a banker's tender guarantee might be worded appears in exhibit 9.1.

Exhibit 9.1: Specimen Banker's Tender Guarantee

WEST BARMID BANK PLC   International Branch
                                         PO Box 64
                                         Main Street
                                         County Town

                                         14th January 1994

The Ministry of Power
Principal City
Anystate

Dear Sirs,

Our Guarantee No G 47/94

<u>Your invitation to Tender 473-26-LB closing date 30 January</u>
<u>1994</u>

With reference to Tender No. 3742 dated 14 January 1994
submitted against the above invitation by – PDB Exports (93)
Ltd 222 Arcade Square, UK Town – we hereby undertake to pay
to you on your first demand on us in writing being received at
this office and bearing our reference Guarantee No. G 47/94
complying with the terms hereof any sum or sums not
exceeding in aggregate £10,000 (ten thousand pounds sterling).
Your demand must state the amount payable and confirm that
PDB Exports (93) Ltd have refused to sign the contract awarded
to them in response to their Tender No. 3742 for the supply of
light standards, control equipment and runway approach
beacons for Amberdash Airport or have withdrawn their tender
prior to adjudication.

Always provided that this undertaking is personal to you and
not assignable and that our liability hereunder is limited to an
aggregate sum not exceeding £10,000 (ten thousand pounds
sterling).

This undertaking shall expire on the 30 May 1994 except in
respect of valid claims received by us on or before that date
after which our undertaking shall become null and void
whether or not it has been returned to us.

This undertaking shall be subject to English law and your
acceptance of the undertaking shall be regarded as your
agreement that you accept the jurisdiction of the Courts of
England to adjudicate on claims thereunder. The undertaking is
also issued subject to ICC Uniform Rules for Demand
Guarantees, ICC Publication No. 458.

Yours faithfully,

A Manager
West Barmid Bank Plc

If a tenderer is successful and signs the resultant contract, the tender guarantee should be released but the buyer will then have a further risk to face: that of the contractor company (as it will now have become) failing to perform the contract terms. This is a more substantial risk in monetary terms than that underlying the tender guarantee. If the contractor ceases work for any reason during the construction of, let us say, a power generating plant, the buyer must find an alternative contractor prepared to complete or, worse, start the entire process of tendering once more, depending on circumstances. As protection against this eventuality the buyer may ask for a banker's performance guarantee, typically for 10 per cent of the contract value payable in the case of the seller failing to perform the contractual terms.

Frequently the requirement for a performance bond from the successful tenderer is mentioned in the invitation documentation and the tender guarantee may not be released until the performance guarantee is received. It is usually a question of fact whether a tenderer has withdrawn or failed to sign a contract (although the reasons for not signing might be arguable), but the position regarding non-performance of a contract is much more difficult and can be a matter of opinion based on varying interpretations of the contract wording and of the quality of work performed or goods or materials supplied.

For this reason contractors are understandably reluctant to instruct their bank to issue a performance guarantee payable on the simple demand of the beneficiary alleging failure to perform as, once again, the contractor will have no opportunity to contest such a claim, even if it is convinced the demand is based on an incorrect interpretation of the contract requirements. In many cases the contractor may have little choice: if the award of a contract is conditional upon the provision of a simple demand banker's guarantee, probably a stipulation in the original invitation to tender documentation, then he must regard this obligation as a prerequisite to tendering or forego the opportunity. However in certain instances it may be possible under the conditions laid down, or following negotiations with the buyer, for a different type of banker's guarantee to be submitted – one which provides for a third party to pronounce on the vexed issue of non-performance of contract. This is known as a conditional or arbitration guarantee and a specimen appears as exhibit 9.2.

Exhibit 9.2: Specimen Conditional or Arbitration Guarantee

WEST BARMID BANK PLC

International Branch
PO Box 64
Main Street
County Town

14th January 1994

The Ministry of Agriculture
Principal City
Anystate

Dear Sirs,

Our Guarantee No G 51/94

We hereby undertake to pay to you any sum or sums not
exceeding in aggregate £50,000 (fifty thousand pounds sterling)
being 10% of the contract price for the supply and erection of
15 horse regenerating plants by Anonymous Construction
Company Plc (the seller) under contract number 45-61-717
dated 14 January 1994 upon your first demand to us in writing
stating that the seller has become liable to pay the sum to you
as a result of non-performance of the contract and has not
made such payment the amount payable and the liability being
evidenced by:

(A) A notarially certified copy of the judgment of a competent
Court of Law in your favour which must accompany your claim
under this guarantee.

or

(B) A notarially certified copy of an arbitrator's award in your
favour which must accompany your claim under this guarantee.

or

(C) A written confirmation addressed to us by the seller stating that the terms of the said contract have not been complied with which must accompany your claim under this guarantee.

Always provided that this undertaking is personal to you and not assignable and that our liability hereunder is limited to an aggregate sum not exceeding £50,000 (fifty thousand pounds sterling).

This undertaking shall expire on the 14 January 1997 except in respect of valid claims received by us on or before that date accompanied by evidence of liability as specified above after which our undertaking shall become null and void whether or not it has been returned to us.

This undertaking shall be subject to English law and your acceptance of the undertaking shall be regarded as your agreement that you accept the jurisdiction of the Courts of England to adjudicate on claims thereunder. The undertaking is also issued to the Uniform Rules for Demand Guarantees, ICC Publication No. 458.

Yours faithfully,

A Manager
West Barmid Bank Plc

The third type of banker's guarantee falling within this general category of contract guarantees is the Advance Payment Guarantee. The circumstances in which the need for this bond arises is where there is an agreement for a single or a series of advance payments to be made under a contract prior to its completion. Frequently the size of such contracts would render it difficult, if not impossible, for the seller to finance all stages of the work, for example under a contract for the supply of a complete plant this would involve delivery, erection and commissioning, before receiving complete settlement. In consequence, contracts are so drawn as to permit 'stage' or 'progress' payments, perhaps on completion of deliveries to site, at two or more stages of erection, and when the plant is operational, with the balance being payable after an agreed period of successful operation.

From the buyer's viewpoint, the outlay on these advance payments increases the risk of loss in the event of non-performance, which has been discussed earlier, and it will request a further banker's guarantee that any or all advance payments will be refunded should non-performance arise. The nature of the guarantee, simple demand or arbitration, will conform to the requirements for the performance bond, differing only in so far as the bank's obligation will be to 'refund' as distinct from making a 'penalty' payment as in the case of either a tender or performance bond which is called.

In the specimen guarantees it has been assumed that in requesting a guarantee the buyer has not specified a wording; it being left to the issuing bank to determine a form which from its experience is appropriate. Should the buyer company object to the terms, it is naturally able to reject the guarantee or require amendments, although in practice most guarantees issued by major banks in such circumstances are acceptable. However it is not unusual for buyers to include in their invitation to tender copies of the wording of any guarantees required, and these can be diverse in content.

It is wise for exporters receiving these invitations to discuss with both their lawyers and their bankers the implications arising as the conditions can be onerous and it is unfortunately not unusual for ambiguities to be included which can lead to distressing results. The bank requested to issue will also have a vested interest in ensuring the intention of the guarantee and the conditions pertaining to claims are crystal clear.

Guarantees Issued by Local Banks

In many countries it is the practice to require guarantees to be issued by a local bank and, even where this is not obligatory, it is quite common for such a request to be made by individual buyers. Reasons for this vary but frequently the buyer feels more secure if his claim is against a bank in his own country in preference to having to pursue action in a foreign environment against a bank which he may or may not know. Such a request involves little difficulty as regards banking implementation but can mean an enhanced liability to the exporter which can normally request the United Kingdom bank to instruct a local bank to issue it; the United Kingdom bank will comply and will indemnify the local bank holding it: 'harmless from all consequences arising' and 'undertaking to pay all such sums as you are required to pay under the terms of your guarantee'. The particular risks to which the exporter is exposed, over and above those connected with the possibility of unfair calling under a simple demand guarantee wherever and by whoever issued, are as follows.

1 It is unlikely although not impossible that the exact wording required in the guarantee is known in advance either to the exporter or to its bank. This means the local bank will be instructed to issue in accordance with the beneficiary's wishes as regards wording subject to such overriding stipulations as the domestic bank, acting on the exporter's instructions, may include in its authority to the local bank. These will probably be confined to the amount, validity and factual particulars of the tender, contract or advance payment to which the guarantee relates. In consequence wording to which the exporter company would have objected had it been aware in advance of the proposed inclusion, is liable to be incorporated. The only effective way in which this can be avoided, remembering that there is seldom time for the local bank to obtain and refer to the United Kingdom bank the beneficiary's suggested wording, is for the exporter to nominate a local agent in the buyer's country which may be empowered to agree wording and lodgement.

2 The law in certain countries renders it impossible to insert an expiry date in the guarantee or provides that it remains in force notwithstanding the inclusion of such a date. The result is that the guarantee liability, which determines that of the exporter towards the bank, will remain indefinitely until such

time as the guarantee is returned for cancellation or the beneficiary confirms release to the issuing bank. A similar end result may occur where a simple demand bond is issued and the beneficiary adopts an 'extend or pay' stance. This consists of a demand for payment by the beneficiary to the issuing bank, which, you will recall, cannot be contested under this type of bond but with the alternative of the bank agreeing to an extension to the validity date. The exporter is in no position to contest and thus must accept the continuance of liability and, incidentally, of bank charges for the guarantee.

3 It is also not unknown for local law or practice to preclude the insertion of a limit to the amount of a guarantee and in such cases the United Kingdom bank may be extremely reluctant to issue as the facility afforded to the exporter in the issuance is similarly unlimited.

4 The comfort of knowing that in the event of legal proceedings in regard to claims these will take place under English law, is lost in the case of a guarantee issued by a bank in the buyer's country which is subject to their laws.

The Exporter's Liability to the Bank

In chapter 7 it was observed that in issuing a letter of credit the bank undertook to make payment to the beneficiary subject to compliance with the terms of the credit and that this undertaking had to be honoured despite any inability to obtain reimbursement from its customer. Thus the bank correctly regarded the opening of the credit as constituting a facility made available to its customer. The same principle applies when a bank issues a guarantee, which in many circumstances covers a situation not dissimilar to a credit, and the bank will therefore consider the customer's creditworthiness before agreeing to the issue and may require security from its principal (the exporter). It will also insist on the completion of a counter-indemnity which confirms both the instruction given and the customer's obligation to reimburse the bank for payments properly made under the guarantee.

The counter-indemnity will only be released at such time as the guarantors are released from their liability to the beneficiary due to the expiry date, the occurrence of any event specified in the guarantee as automatically triggering expiry, the return for cancellation of the guarantee or the beneficiary's written confirmation of release. The amount of the customer's liability under the counter-indemnity may however be decreased progressively where guarantees provide for reductions in the guarantor's liability towards the beneficiaries to be similarly decreased. For example a guarantee covering performance of a contract to supply a specified quantity of goods might contain a clause authorizing progressive reductions upon production to the guarantor of signed acceptance notes evidencing the receipt of partial deliveries.

The International Chamber of Commerce published in 1992 the *ICC Uniform Rules for Demand Guarantees* which seeks to provide a similar internationally accepted code of practice for demand guarantees to that available to users of documentary credits through the uniform credit practices. Those involved with guarantees are recommended to acquire copies. The rules cover many of the problem areas which have been discussed and their value lies in concentrating the attention of exporters on the dangers inherent in the issue of demand guarantees rather than attempting to minimize those risks. This is indicative of the common sense approach of the experts brought together by the Chamber in recognizing that the demand guarantee is normally the alternative to a cash deposit or retention and, as such, must provide the same degree of protection to the beneficiary as would be attainable were those methods of security to be adopted.

There are however several useful rules designed to avoid friction between the parties due to lack of information or unreasonable haste. For example it has long been a source of irritation to exporters that the beneficiary's demand for payment under a performance or advance payment guarantee was not required to stipulate, even in general terms, the nature of the alleged breach of contract. This is now remedied in respect of guarantees issued subject to the Uniform Rules but it must be stressed that guarantees, like documentary credits, are concerned only with the presentation of documents such as the beneficiary's written demand, and not with the underlying commercial contract for the supply of goods or services. It follows therefore that whatever the nature of the alleged breach the guarantor is not concerned as to its authenticity; merely that if the guarantee requires it to be specified in any demand that requirement is fulfilled. The importance of any guarantee including an expiry date or other indication of the documentation which upon presentation will constitute an end to liability, is also confirmed in the rules but this will not of course alter any conditions under the governing law which may restrict or even render academic the validity provisions of the guarantee.

Time constraints which might be considered unreasonable are typified by the inclusion in the rules of agreement that where the beneficiary submits an 'extend or pay' demand as explained earlier in this chapter, payment shall be suspended until the principal and beneficiary have had a reasonable time to reach agreement on the extension. The intention is clearly to avoid undue pressurization of the exporter to extend while still recognizing that the beneficiary is within his rights under the guarantee in making this type of demand. Readers who may encounter this situation are strongly advised to refer to the wording of Article 26 of the rules.

Alternative methods to the bank guarantee for providing the security required by the buyer inviting tenders or awarding a contract do exist, although their use is normally confined to countries where the issue by banks of this type of guarantee is not permissable or acceptable. In chapter 7 we discussed one such alternative, the stand-by letter of credit payable against the beneficiary's statement that the tenderer or contractor had failed to observe the terms of the tender or to perform the contract as appropriate. The only additional comment necessary at this stage is that in interpreting practice in respect of these credits it is Uniform Customs and Practice for Documentary Credits (UCP) which will apply and not Uniform Rules for Demand Guarantees. The latter however apply equally to the second alternative, that of a guarantee issued by a fidelity or insurance company which will normally be in similar terms to that of a bank.

The third and final alternative is a reminder that any form of security in lieu of a cash deposit or retention must possess the same capacity for ready realization by the beneficiary; exporters may occasionally be asked to support tenders by a certified cheque from a bank; these are cheques issued by a bank on itself payable to the buyer and can be encashed at any time. The exporter agreeing to this request has minimal protection against any unfair encashment and the practice is not covered by Uniform Rules. It is recommended that such requests be discussed by a United Kingdom exporter with his bank in order that the implications of liability may be understood.

Indemnities Securing the Release of Goods

The best known type of banker's indemnity is that issued to a shipping company enabling it to release goods to an importer without the production of a document of title – a bill of lading. The indemnity is an agreement directly between the bank and the shipping company and is not dependent on the importer performing or not performing any act. It is based, as are most indemnities and guarantees, on consideration; that is the giving of some form of value by way of deed or service against which the indemnity or guarantee is issued. In this case consideration is the delivery of goods other than against a document of title, and the indemnity will hold the beneficiary (shipping company) harmless from all consequences arising from that delivery, including the reimbursement of any losses which the company may sustain as a result of any claim pursued by a holder of the bill of lading who is not the party to whom the goods have been released. This type of indemnity is normally of short duration and will be released when the delayed bills of lading are received and surrendered to the shipping company. Frequently the document is signed jointly by the bank and the buyer, and it will not contain an amount as it is not possible to quantify the loss which might be incurred were wrongful delivery to be established.

Bank Guarantees in Support of Loan or Overdraft Facilities

Exporters may have a number of reasons for requiring to borrow from banks outside their own country either by way of overdraft or fixed loan. In chapter 4 it was observed that borrowing could be arranged in a wide range of currencies and was a prudent course of action provided it was realized that repayment must be in the currency borrowed. If the borrower had no source of that currency and were to rely on converting an appropriate amount of an alternative currency at the maturity of the loan a serious exchange risk would of course arise. Among the more common reasons for such borrowing are the following.

1 To provide working capital for a subsidiary company over-seas in which case the borrowing would probably be in the name of that company but would initially require the support of the parent.
2 To provide funds to support staff temporarily seconded to an overseas country to manage a substantial construction or similar project.
3 To fund the local costs incurred in a major project, for example the labour force recruited in the buyer's country. Often this is particularly desirable as some less developed countries insist on a portion of the purchase price being expressed in local (and non-convertible) currency, and these monies when received can be applied in repayment of the borrowing.

In many instances the borrower will be unknown to the lending bank and in most cases will have no customer relationship on which creditworthiness can be assessed. Thus to obtain the facilities might be both difficult and expensive unless acceptable security is offered. The United Kingdom based company will therefore request its bankers to issue their guarantee in favour of the lending bank which should ensure the facilities are ob-tained at a fine margin over interest rates pertaining. Exhibits 9.3 and 9.4 show a typical format for guarantees covering overdraft facilities and a fixed term loan respectively.

Exhibit 9.3: Specimen Overdraft Facility Guarantee

HAMPSHIRE COUNTY BANK PLC

Overseas Branch
PO Box 41
High Street
County Town

14th January 1994

The Rural Enterprise Bank
74 Oswaldgate
Springbokvale
South Africa

Dear Sirs,

Our Guarantee No 52G

Please grant to PDB Associates (South Africa) overdraft facilities subject to your having the right to cancel such facilities at any time and our having the right to determine our liability hereunder by notice in writing upon receipt of which no further advances are to be made without recourse to us.

We hereby undertake to pay to you the outstanding balance under the above facilities not exceeding South African Rands 100,000 plus interest from the date of this undertaking or that upon which the facilities are made available (whichever shall be the later) until the date of payment to you upon receipt of your first demand in writing confirming that PDB Associates (South Africa) have failed to make repayment of the outstanding balance despite your having claimed such repayment from them.

It is understood that this undertaking is personal to you and not assignable.

Our liability shall not exceed in aggregate the sum of 100,000 South African Rands (one hundred thousand South African Rands) plus interest. Such liability shall terminate on the 20th January 1995 or on any earlier date upon which any notice of termination given by us shall be received by you except in respect of written demands from yourselves complying with the terms of this undertaking received by us not later than 30 days from that date. Thereafter this undertaking whether or not returned to us shall become null and void.

This undertaking shall be governed by English law and the Courts of England shall have jurisdiction to arbitrate on any claim; your acceptance of this undertaking being your confirmation that you submit to such jurisdiction.

We await your advice that the facilities have been granted to PDB Associates (South Africa).

Yours faithfully,

A Manager
Hampshire County Bank Plc

Exhibit 9.4: Specimen Fixed Term Loan Guarantee

HAMPSHIRE COUNTY BANK PLC

Overseas Branch
PO Box 41
High Street
County Town

14th January 1994

The Rural Enterprise Bank
74 Oswaldgate
Springbokvale
South Africa

Dear Sirs,

Our Guarantee No 63G

Please grant to PDB Associates (South Africa) a loan facility until the 20 January 1995. In consideration of your granting this facility we undertake to pay to you a sum or sums not exceeding in aggregate South African Rands 100,000 (one hundred thousand South African Rands) inclusive of interest calculated on amounts not exceeding the above sum from the date of this undertaking or that upon which the loan facility is granted (whichever shall be the later) until the date of payment to you upon receipt of your first demand in writing confirming that PDB Associates (South Africa) have failed to make repayment of the loan on or before the 20 January 1995.

It is understood that this undertaking is personal to you and is not assignable.

Our liability shall not exceed in aggregate the sum of 100,000 South African Rands (one hundred thousand South African Rands) inclusive of interest.

Such liability shall terminate on the 10th February 1995 except in respect of written demands from yourselves complying with the terms of this undertaking received by us not later than that date after which this undertaking whether or not returned to us shall become null and void.

This undertaking shall be governed by English law and the Courts of England shall have jurisdiction to arbitrate on any claim; your acceptance of this undertaking being your confirmation that you submit to such jurisdiction.

We await your advice that the loan facilities have been granted to PDB Associates (South Africa).

Yours faithfully,

A Manager
Hampshire County Bank Plc

A number of the provisions appearing in exhibits 9.3 and 9.4 are worthy of particular comment.

The liability of the guarantor is expressed in the same currency as that in which the overdraft or loan is to be granted. Although there is no technical objection to the guarantor specifying his liability in sterling, a practical difficulty is that of determining a realistic rate of exchange to be applied in calculating the amount. If the sterling figure is regarded as too low by the guaranteed bank it may be rejected or a downward adjustment made to the amount of the facilities offered. Should the sterling figure be unduly inflated the customer of the guarantor bank may consider the liability and any consequent security required to be excessive. In any event the rate of exchange applied can be no more than a guess based on those quoted spot or forward at the time the guarantee is issued; the rate which will apply on the date of any claim being received is unknown.

The problem posed above arises solely because the guarantee is against the possible and not undoubted arising of a particular occurrence; the lending bank being unable to obtain repayment of the loan or overdraft from the borrower and thus reverting to the guarantor. If this was a certainty then the guarantor could enter into a forward exchange contract provided it was known the facilities were to terminate on a fixed date or between two specified future dates for which forward quotes were obtainable and that the currency of the facilities was convertible. In fact it is by no means a certainty that a claim will be made; quite the contrary, as in the vast majority of cases the borrower will repay and the guarantee will be released. It is for this reason that the guarantees in exhibits 9.3 and 9.4 are worded to make clear that the lending bank cannot make claim on the guarantor bank until repayment has been demanded from the borrower and refused.

The guarantees do not specify the amount of the facilities which the Rural Enterprise Bank will make available, only the amount which the Hampshire County Bank will guarantee. Note that in exhibit 9.3 the guaranteed amount is plus interest whereas in exhibit 9.4 it is inclusive of interest. In the latter case if the Rural Enterprise Bank wishes to be covered 100 per cent by the guarantee in respect of funds lent, it will make a loan of less than 100,000 Rands whereas it can achieve 100 per cent cover in the former case, even if the full 100,000 Rands represents the amount of the overdraft facilities offered.

Although most bank guarantees of this type cover overdraft or loan facilities it is possible for other facilities such as the discounting of bills of exchange to be covered by a simple adaptation of the wording.

Custom Clearance Guarantees

There are a number of other types of bank guarantees designed to cover various contingencies but only one, the guarantee given to enable customs clearance, is of direct benefit to the exporter. The circumstances in which this guarantee is required are when an exporter decides to participate in an exhibition abroad. There are a number of ways in which the goods to be exhibited can be cleared through customs at the place of entry without immediate payment of duty and this is desirable as the exporter may or may not require to return them to his own country. Obviously this will depend on whether a sale is effected during the exhibition in which case delivery can be made without returning goods but any duty payable will be immediately due.

If a bank guarantee is the chosen method it will undertake in consideration of the goods being admitted without payment of duty, to settle such duty as may be payable in the event of the goods failing to be re-exported within a specified time. Thus if the customs authorities having monitored the entry are without evidence by the date specified of re-exportation having been effected, they may claim under the guarantee without further formality.

10

Finance for International Trade

This chapter heading should not mislead the reader into assuming that the problem of financing exports and imports is basically different from that presented to the buyers and sellers operating exclusively in their home market. It is not; some of the methods used to finance international trade are not appropriate to domestic transactions, others might be unusual in that context but the majority are common to both, as are the principles applied by lenders.

In reviewing the options it is necessary to differentiate between the needs of the potential exporter in developing markets (or those of an existing exporter seeking to widen the range of markets supplied) and the quest for finance to cover the period between the conclusion of an export contract and the settlement. The former involves all the customary risks associated with a new venture. Is there the expertise? Have all the risks of taking on a new aspect of trading been evaluated? And is the projected rate of progress towards a break-even point realistic? To mention but a few. The latter, the quest for finance to cover the period between the conclusion of an export contract and the settlement, also includes the lender's assessing the exporter's judgement and ability to supply goods but additionally there is the buyer to be considered and, most importantly, the proposition for finance is now characterized by the movement of tangible assets; the goods.

Bank Finance to Establish Export Markets – Overdrafts and Loans

The prudent trader will endeavour to self-finance from its company's resources as great a proportion as possible of the costs of establishing or expanding an export market prior to any business being contracted. Of course lenders will consider providing assistance for set-up costs, usually by way of overdraft or fixed term loan, but the degree of risk is significant and, depending on the individual circumstances of the borrower including security available, may be measured in the interest margin applied. If it is necessary to seek financial support, propositions should invariably include the following.

1 A cash flow forecast indicating the anticipated period necessary to recoup the set-up costs through sales.
2 The level of expertise in international trading, if any, already available to the company and details of the proposals designed to increase this level to that necessary to achieve the stated objectives. This may be attained by recruiting staff with the appropriate experience or by employing outside expert assistance, for example a freight forwarder to handle transportation, or both.
3 The results of any preliminary market research undertaken to verify that a commercial demand for the company's products exists at a price which is both competitive and profitable.
4 The spread of markets to be explored; as we observed in chapter 2 'country risk' varies greatly and costs incurred in researching unpromising markets may be ill-spent.
5 The results of preliminary enquiries on the period of credit likely to be required in overseas markets and the implications for the borrower's cash flow. A statement of the company's intentions regarding credit control procedures would also be a welcome addition.

Remember that, contrary to media suggestions, bank managers' horns and forked tails appear very infrequently in dealing with customers and undoubtedly that frequency is still further reduced when they are invited to share in the logical reasoning which has led up to a request for facilities. Although considerable success has marked the 'credit scoring' method of assessing loans for individuals, the evaluation of requests for corporate facilities is still a matter for the personal judgement of the sanctioning official who may be the branch manager, corporate manager, or more senior management according to the circumstances and amount required. In reaching a decision that official is able to call on specialist management experienced in international trade finance and this is a further reason for exporters to devote adequate time to presenting a case which is professional in its content.

Bank Finance from Contract to Payment – Overdrafts and Loans

The need for a well reasoned approach is no less important when the facilities are to cover finance for a particular export or series of overseas sales. In practice many companies request working capital for their business as a whole without differentiating between domestic and overseas trade; facilities where granted are on balance sheet considerations. This must be a choice for the finance director and the only comment from experience is that multi-purpose borrowing should not have the indirect result of lessening the need for constant monitoring of the export outstandings. In this context of finance and the need to protect cash flow read once again the early part of chapter 5, in which were observed the reasons for past losses by exporters, and it will be apparent that the possibilities of eroding hard won facilities through mistakes and lack of credit control are particularly noticeable in relation to overseas trade.

If a company is seeking overdraft or loan facilities specifically for export contracts the lender is concerned not only with the borrower's standing, unless taking the narrow view that recourse to him will ultimately achieve repayment, but with the 'buyer risk' the borrower is incurring in those contracts and the efficiency of its credit control. It is in the quality of an exporter's order book and his ability to achieve settlement in good time that the lender's confidence in repayments rests. The approach for facilities should include supportive material as follows.

1 Details of the proposed contracts, buyers, amounts, credit terms required and the results of status enquiries. The bank shares your reliance on these buyers.
2 Confirmation that the supply of goods within the promised delivery dates presents no problem in productive capacity or the supply of necessary raw materials or components. The bank will be aware of your general order book and capacity but it is not an expert in the trade and the possible specific problems resulting from an overseas order which might not be for standard goods.
3 The proposed method of payment to be adopted including the buyer's reactions or agreement.
4 A cash flow prediction if the finance is to cover a series of contracts.

The advantages of the exporter acquainting the bank with its plans and, where applicable, apprehensions, extend beyond enhancing the likelihood of receiving a favourable decision on the application for finance. In their international business, banks acquire a significant amount of knowledge of overseas controls and, in their own interests, keep this up-to-date through regular contacts with their branches abroad or correspondent bank management. To this is added a continuous flow of international trade settlements using a wide selection of methods of payment which results in the bank being well informed of the pitfalls, how they can be avoided and the actions desirable if the unexpected occurs.

All of the non-confidential information obtained is available to customers and, in providing it, the bank is both assisting the smooth running of the customer's business and, if it is providing finance, protecting its own investment. From painful experience I can appreciate the frustration and distress to both bank and customers when the former is kept unaware of export initiatives until a major financial problem arises which might have been avoided by earlier discussion; the customer struggles to familiarize itself with the complexities of international trade payments oblivious of the ability of the bank to assist. The specialists mentioned earlier, who may assist a sanctioning official con-sidering a loan proposition, are equally available to corporate customers entering or expanding exporting. Use them through an introduction readily obtainable from your local branch or corporate manager.

Security Considerations – Credit Insurance Cover

It is not within the aims of this book to consider the reasoning behind the banks' requests for security or the nature of that security, except where it is peculiar to international trade. The first type of security falling within this category is a policy issued by a credit insurer covering goods which are to be exported. As the role played by credit insurance in facilitating finance is frequently different in the case of sales on credit terms up to 180 days (short term) to that applying to sales involving longer credit terms, we will consider these categories separately.

The conditions of cover provided by credit insurers for exports sold on short term credit were described in chapter 2 and are typified by the international guarantee of NCM which is the main insurer in this field. This type of policy can feature in a number of ways in providing security for exporters wishing to obtain finance. The policy may include a 'nomination of loss payee' which is a party to whom the insurer will pay monies resulting from a claim. The party is nominated by the exporter and will, or course, be the provider of the required finance. The position is similar to the assignment of policies, giving banks or other lenders supporting security for loans, which was the practice when short term credit insurance was primarily effected through the Export Credits Guarantee Department (ECGD) from whom the business was acquired by NCM. Although there are legal distinctions between 'assignment' and 'nomination of loss payee' most lenders are prepared to accord similar treatment to would be borrowers offering policies with either provision.

At various times during the past 20 years efforts have been made to integrate bank lending with credit insurance short term cover in a more direct way, but these endeavours have met with only limited success. Up to 1987 ECGD provided comprehensive banker's guarantees which effectively gave banks an undertaking that in the event of repayment of loans or overdrafts being prevented by the results of risks covered by the credit insurance policy, ECGD would reimburse the bank, thus removing the need for recourse to the borrower. This enabled the bank to offer preferential margins over interest rates in consideration of the enhanced security. Following the demise of these guarantees banks introduced a variety of schemes intended to preserve the principle of increased flexibility in short term lending to customers being possible if an acceptable credit insurance policy was available to increase security. The policy could be either that in force between the exporting customer and the insurer or one which the bank itself took out.

Another variation was for some banks to take out policies which were managed by specialist firms versed in credit insurance, although the policy itself was in the bank's name. At the time of writing a few banks continue to operate these schemes but many have discontinued. So far as I am aware no reasons have been given publicly for the relative failure of these schemes, but one suspects that the administration costs in times of stringent cost control by the banks have been a major factor and that the demand from borrowers was not as high as envisaged. The saving, if any, on interest rate margins under the Export Credits Guarantee Department guarantees were very small for blue chip borrowers who rarely used the facilities, and the main beneficiaries costwise were small company borrowers whose normal borrowing attracted a significant margin. Unfortunately due to recessionary factors many of the latter failed to survive. Another significant influence was the presence of two risks to the lender notwithstanding the credit insurance cover.

The first is that the insurance will naturally exclude any losses arising from the failure of the exporter to perform the terms of his commercial contract with the buyer; not unknown when the borrower may be a firm inexperienced in export matters. The second is a failure by the exporter to comply with any warranties or other conditions of the insurance cover; a risk which can be avoided by a close monitoring but at an appreciable cost. I would agree with Brian White in his informative guide to trade finance by bankers, that these risks render questionable any statement that lending under such schemes is 'without recourse'.

Before leaving the short term credit category it should be observed that banks have suggested to many borrowers previously using the schemes detailed above, that their requirements may be met by using the export facilities offered by factors. Many factoring companies are subsidiaries of banks and the periodic reassessment of whether a particular demand is best met by one company or another within the group can be beneficial to both lender and borrower. Factoring companies operate using credit insurance and, as we shall note when considering their activities later in this chapter, they offer particular advantages to borrowers (whose sale patterns suit a factoring scenario) in times of recession and lending stringency.

The exporter seeking finance for sales with credit terms of two years or more and wishing to utilize credit insurance by way of security is offered a different and more complex range of options. The first should not be included in a summary of facilities available to an exporter (supplier) as it is not strictly for its use but that of the overseas buyer. We shall however include it in our survey as, in practice, it provides an answer to the finance problem faced by exporters whose contracts meet the requirements albeit by enabling cash terms to be enjoyed. The facilities, known as 'buyer credit', operate by means of a loan from a British bank through a bank in the purchaser's country to the buyer, the United Kingdom being guaranteed 100 per cent by the Export Credits Guarantee Department in the event of repayment not being made by the borrower. The interest rate on the loan is determined by the Department and is in accordance with a range of rates agreed internationally through the Organisations for Economic Co-operation and Development (OECD) which are termed 'consensus rates'.

Interest is the responsibility of the buyer, the British bank's recourse is to the ECGD and the Department in turn has recourse to the buyer and not the exporter (supplier). Thus the

latter may rely on 'cash terms' in the knowledge that the buyer
is able to obtain the credit he requires by way of a loan on
at least as favourable terms as would have applied had the
exporter been able and willing to seek finance at the buyer's
expense. The sole obligation for which the exporter company
must make provision is responsibility to meet the premium
charged by ECGD and it should ascertain the amount involved
in order to include it in the price. Beyond this monetary obligation the exporter must, as with any other credit insurance,
ensure that the terms of the commercial contract are correctly
completed; that is if it should fail to do so, ECGD would have
recourse on the ground that the policy warranty has been
breached.

The paperwork and detail involved in 'buyer credit' are necessarily substantial and in consequence this form of finance is
normally confined to commercial contracts to a value in excess
of £5m; to ensure good faith on the part of the buyer a down
payment, typically 15-20 per cent, is required with the balance
met from the loan arrangement.

The second option is a derivative of buyer credit but applies
in respect of trade between the United Kingdom and selected
overseas markets where a general purpose line of credit is
agreed by ECGD. Under this type of arrangement the United
Kingdom bank agrees with a bank in the country to which the
line of credit is extended, to finance United Kingdom suppliers
with contracts with overseas buyers. The minimum amount for
eligible contracts is publicized, usually US$25,000, and thus
quite modest exporters may benefit unlike the normal buyer
credit described above which, by reason of the high minimum,
is of interest only to substantial exporters. A similar facility used
for financing specific projects, usually of considerable size but
frequently involving a large number of suppliers whose contribution is again of modest contract value, is the project line of
credit.

A distinctly different concept of assisting exporters through
credit insurance is the Supplier Credit Financing Facility of ECGD
which also applies to sales overseas on medium term credit but
operates to facilitate the obtaining of finance by the exporter,
not the buyer. The procedure is as follows: The exporter's bank

will normally purchase accepted bills of exchange, or promissory notes issued by the buyer without recourse to the exporter as it relies on a 100 per cent guarantee from ECGD to cover any payment default arising after the purchase. Guarantees require that the credit period should be at least two years, that the lending bank be authorized under the Banking Act 1987 and acceptable to ECGD and that finance provided should not exceed 85 per cent of the contract, the balance being payable prior to the commencement of the credit period by the buyer to the exporter. It should be stressed that the Supplier Credit Financing Facility covers only the finance element and exporters may well decide to cover pre-finance risks by securing additional credit insurance as set out in chapter 2.

Security Considerations – Bills of Exchange

In chapter 6 we considered the role of a bill of exchange as a method of payment between buyer and exporter; let us now widen that examination to discover how that document may assist the exporter to obtain finance. You will recall that we learnt that in cases where credit was extended to the buyer, the bill of exchange would indicate it was payable at an appropriate number of days after sight and that in order to obtain shipping documents from the collecting or presenting bank the buyer must 'accept' the bill. This was achieved by his writing 'accepted payable . . .' (the date calculated as that of maturity according to the number of days after sight) and signing the acceptance across the face of the bill. If the exporter requires finance he may, as an alternative to asking his bank (the remitting bank) to collect the bill, ask it to negotiate. If the bank is prepared to approve this request they will pay the exporter the face value of the bill less a discount which will represent interest for the time they are out of funds until payment is received upon maturity of the usance bill plus the margin over cost.

Normally the bank will reserve the right to have recourse to the exporter should the buyer dishonour the bill although in certain cases, as we shall discover later, negotiation may be without recourse. As the bank is regarding the bill as security, in whole or in part, and is usually maintaining recourse it is therefore examining with care the financial standing of both drawee (buyer) and the drawer (exporter). It may also require a Letter of Hypothecation by which the exporter authorizes the bank to sell the goods to reimburse itself in the event of the bill being dishonoured but, as this document is more widely used in regard to finance for imports, we will consider it further under that heading.

An exporter may consider, after making the necessary enquiries, a need for a guarantee of a bank that the bill of exchange will be paid, but does not wish to request a letter of credit. In continental Europe this requirement can be met by the bank adding its 'aval' to the bill. This involves the bank endorsing the bill (pour aval) thereby giving its guarantee of payment. Avalized bills become, for practical purposes, identical with those drawn on, and accepted by, banks in that they are discountable at fine rates and holders will normally look to the bank and not the drawee for payment. It is not within our scope to consider the legal situation in the United Kingdom regarding the 'avalization' of bills; sufficient to say that it is obscure and that in consequence United Kingdom banks do not normally adopt the practice although there is a continuing dialogue regarding the merits of achieving an internationally acceptable solution.

A usage of bills of exchange which often confuses students occurs under a banker's acceptance credit. The name itself contributes to misunderstandings; many mistake it for a type of documentary credit which it is not. Bills which we have considered thus far, including those drawn under documentary credits, are directly related to a contract or contracts of sale and provide a means of settlement between buyer and seller. Banker's acceptance credits are normally related indirectly to a trade deal between buyer and exporter but are the means of achieving finance for the exporter and not settlement between the trading partners. The exporter is permitted by the bank to draw on it bills of exchange which are then accepted and returned to the exporter who can arrange discount in the market at the same fine rates which are applicable to any other form of bank acceptances (bank bills).

The banks specializing in this type of finance are not the United Kingdom clearing banks, whose financing role is to lend money, but the merchant banks or accepting houses which are members of the Accepting House Committee and Issuing Houses Association. Members of this association include many whose histories date from the 17th or 18th century, and their names are their stock-in-trade being sufficient as acceptors to ensure a 'first class' bill. It is interesting to reflect that the inter-relation between the clearing banks, merchant banks and discount houses is characteristic of the manner in which various financial institutions – each with a distinctive discipline – combine to provide a flexibility in financing methods which is among the reasons for London remaining the prime international finance centre.

Forfaiting

It is logical that this method of finance should be considered immediately following an examination of the general role played by the bill of exchange in trade finance; forfaiting operates on the basis that a bill, or series of bills, is the method of payment between exporter and buyer. It is a system which is designed to meet the demand from exporters of capital goods on credit terms between one and five years (sometimes extended to seven years) for finance on a 'without recourse' basis.

Forfaiting originated in continental Europe and was devised by the Swiss banks, who still specialize in this form of finance, but is available to British exporters through British banking groups. Its continental origins resulted from the absence of any equivalent of supplier or buyer credit schemes similar to those offered by the Export Credits Guarantee Department and the long standing acceptance on the continent of the practice of banks avalizing bills of exchange. While bills form a large pro-portion of forfaiting operations it is also common for a buyer to issue a promissory note which is similarly purchased without recourse by the forfaiter. Whether bills or promissory notes are used it is customary for them to be drawn in a series over the life of the contract which will provide for payment by instalments. Thus over a 5 year contract bills or notes might mature at 6, 12, 18, 24 and 30 months respectively and so on with the last bill payable at the conclusion of the contract.

To illustrate forfaiting let us take a typical example. An exporter has contracted to supply capital goods to an overseas buyer with a credit period of five years and payment is to be through 10 equal instalments at intervals of six months. The importer accepts 10 bills of exchange covering these half-yearly instalments and these are avalized by a first class international bank acceptable to the forfaiting bank. As the forfaiting bank will obviously look to the avalizing bank for payment, the latter will have to be assured of the creditworthiness of the buyer for whom it is assuming liability and the acceptability of any country risk involved.

The bills may be expressed in any currency acceptable to the forfaiting bank although it is normal to require one of the major currencies with unlimited acceptability in financial centres worldwide. The forfaiting bank will purchase the avalized bills from the exporter at a price which will reflect the interest over the period and a margin commensurate with the risk undertaken, both of which will appear in the discount against face value. This purchase will be without recourse to the seller (exporter). Upon maturity of each bill the forfaiting bank will present it for payment unless it has, prior to maturity, been rediscounted in the market in which case presentation is made by the holder at maturity.

Costs of forfaiting may be high where documentary formalities are onerous but it has many advantages for the exporter including the removal of collection problems and exchange risks; the avoidance of contingent liabilities which would arise with finance obtained on a 'with recourse' basis and a useful system by which finance can be obtained for medium term sales to buyers particularly in the European Community, where ECGD facilities are not on offer. It should be added that the forfaiter will often require that some portion of the purchase price of the goods be paid in advance (typically 15-20 per cent) and that the forfaiting arrangements be restricted to the balance which is not dissimilar to the ECGD requirements mentioned earlier.

Factoring

If we look to Switzerland for the origins of forfaiting, it is to the United States we must turn for the growth of factoring and it is only over the last 10-15 years that a considerable growth in this type of finance in the United Kingdom has taken place. Unlike the operations described earlier in this chapter, factoring offers a service to its client which does not necessarily include the provision of finance although it is correct to say that its increasing appeal over the period of economic recession owes much to the ability of clients to obtain assistance of this nature.

Factoring companies, many of which are associated with banks, offer to buy the book debts of a client at a price, to arrange collection and to lift from the shoulders of the client the burdens of status enquiries, credit control, and foreign exchange risk. It may also in some instances attend to shipping or forwarding of the goods. The result is that the client is able to concentrate on marketing, research and production, having no further need for a sales ledger handling department and is also saved the costs of staff who would be essential for such a department. It is also probable that the experience of the factors, many of whom are part of international groups, will result in a more efficient and speedy collection of outstandings than could be achieved by an inexperienced exporter, although it should not be assumed factoring is only for the small or new exporter; many large companies selling consumer goods on credit terms of up to 180 days find it cost effective and convenient to use factors.

The factor charges a commission, based on turnover, for taking over a sales ledger and in calculating the charge is mindful of the work load reflected in average invoice size, number of debtors, and the range of countries to which the client exports with the consequent risk. One of the perceived difficulties by some companies considering the use of a factor is that, if known to the buyer, it might have had an adverse effect on the sales relationship. To meet this situation some factors offer an invoice discounting service whereby the sales ledger remains within the control of the client while the factor underwrites the debts and agrees to advance against invoices. This is a further indication of the flexibility and varied nature of factoring; it may be used by different clients for differing types of service.

The finance provided by factors may be with recourse or without recourse according to the client's requirements and the nature of individual propositions. With recourse factoring enables the client to receive advances against invoices and is similar to a bank making advances against bills of exchange in course of collection. Should the buyer fail to pay, the client must refund the advance and there is no assumption of credit risk or debt insurance by the factor. In contrast, without recourse factoring involves the factor in providing debt insurance thus absolving his client from credit risk.

Among other advantages of factoring are:

1 it often enables a client to offer open account terms to the buyer in circumstances where without factoring a more secure method of payment would be requested;
2 the advances available against invoices can be for up to 80 per cent with the balance payable on settlement by the buyer;
3 companies which have a highly seasonal export business may be able to achieve a more even cash flow by using a factor; and
4 it can be extremely valuable to a company which is rapidly increasing its overseas business and might experience difficulty in obtaining traditional overdraft or loan facilities from its bankers, particularly in times of recession or credit stringency.

Other Sources of Finance

Export houses

Export houses play an important role in British exports which is much wider than that of providing finance. Most are specialists, many concentrating on particular countries or products, and exporters can obtain details from the British Export Houses Association to which the vast majority of export houses belong.

The nature of services offered by an export house (export merchant or buying agent) vary but a common factor is that they all have considerable knowledge of, and experience in fulfilling, buyers needs and in some cases actually act as their agents for purchasing in the United Kingdom. Let us examine each of the methods by which these houses seek to assist British exporters.

If their client wishes to avoid all the risks and duties normally associated with exporting including not only credit risk, administration and credit control, which were often undertaken by a factor, but also sales promotion and after sales service, an export house may be prepared to undertake some or all of these responsibilities. The client remains the principal but elects to pay the house to perform virtually all functions normally involved in export in preference to incurring the costs himself. There is no magic formula to determine at what point or in what circumstances this becomes a wise decision; all that can be said is that it is part of our duty in surveying the financial aspects of exporting to stress that a continuing review of the most cost effective way of handling each and every facet is a prudent course.

An export house may act as principal, buying the goods from an exporter and effectively converting the sale from its point of view to a domestic one with obvious benefits to his finances. The house then sells to an overseas buyer, frequently using its expertise to facilitate the choice of buyer or, in some instances, in satisfaction of a known requirement. An interesting and important application of this method is where the client seeks the assistance of the export house in finding a market for goods offered under countertrade (see chapter 1).

Houses may act for overseas importers (buyers) on a commission basis; in such cases they are known as confirming houses as they 'confirm' the buyer's order to the United Kingdom exporter. When acting in this manner they will be the principal in the transaction paying the exporter against goods for shipment and themselves arranging any credit terms which may be required by the buyer. Thus the exporter is in practice receiving finance in so far as he is not required to bear the costs of the buyer's credit requirements.

Export finance houses

These are institutions which provide finance to exporters by making immediate payment against shipping documents on a without recourse basis, having taken out credit insurance cover on the buyer. The credit terms which a particular house is prepared to finance vary, some houses preferring short term (up to 180 days) while others will consider medium term up to 5 years.

International credit unions

In a number of countries, including the United Kingdom, certain banks and finance houses have joined together to form international trade associations which seek to establish reciprocal arrangements whereby local finance is provided to an importer who is trading with an exporter in the country of another member. The arrangements are activated by the exporter, who has received an approach from the potential buyer for extended credit or instalment payments. The request is conveyed to the finance house in the exporter's country which will determine through its associates in the importer's country if the requested terms are acceptable for local finance with particular reference to the importer's credit standing.

If the response is favourable the conditions are conveyed to the exporter who notifies the importer; the chain is completed by the latter contacting the local finance house from whom the finance is received. The benefits to the exporter are that it may be able to achieve business which would otherwise be difficult to secure due to the envisaged payment terms and the financing is facilitated by the houses in both countries being in close contact (through mutual membership of the International Credit Union) throughout the transaction.

Finance for Imports

Why, you may ask, are we including in a book designed to explain to exporters the financial aspects of international trading, information on finance available to importers? The answer is that to be professional in his approach to finance the exporter needs to be aware of the problems of his buyer and possible solutions. There will be occasions, such as those outlined in our consideration of International Credit Unions, where a particular transaction or series of transactions is best facilitated by finance to the importer and not the exporter; each set of circumstances warrants individual research.

Naturally many importers will take advantage of the same range of overdraft and loan facilities as we have identified as being available to exporters. Similarly the extension of a period of credit by the exporter through open account terms, usance drafts on the buyer or the arranging of a usance letter of credit provide 'finance' or assistance in managing cash flow to the importer. It will also, in suitable cases, benefit from buyer credit made available through the Export Credits Guarantee Department at the instigation of the exporter while, indirectly, supplier credit through ECGD will assist by enabling the exporter to quote favourable credit terms. Apart from these alternatives, there is one method of finance which is often available to importers and has characteristics which set it apart from other methods: the produce loan.

We have observed when discussing letters of credit that banks undertaking liabilities such as the opening of documentary credit will include in the application form to be signed by the importer an agreement that the documents, the goods, all proceeds of sale and of insurance together with the applicant's rights as an unpaid seller shall be security to the bank for such liabilities as they assume. When an importer requests finance either to cover the purchase from overseas or from the date he receives the goods until such time as they are on-sold to the end-buyer, the bank may well require the security of the goods against the advance which will be made as a specific loan. This does not mean the bank will be unmindful of the other criteria for lending, the character and creditworthiness of the borrower, and the goods will provide only one component of security. Indeed banks in considering goods as security are extremely cautious; the merchandise must be readily saleable even on a 'forced sale' basis and banks prefer commodities or other goods for which there is an established market throughout the year. However manufactured goods may be accepted as security but in all cases the lender will evaluate the likely price in the event of a forced sale and will not lend any amount approaching 100 per cent of the invoiced price.

The form of security will vary according to whether the goods are in transit or are already in the possession of the buyer. In the former event documents of title will be deposited, in the latter the goods will be warehoused in the bank's name with a warrant or receipt deposited. The documents or goods are then stated to be 'pledged' to the bank but this is formalized by the borrower which is required to complete a letter of hypothecation which confers upon the bank the right to sell the goods should default occur on the loan. This document covers sale proceeds as well as those resulting from insurance claims and by signing the borrower also undertakes:

1 that the goods are readily marketable and have a value as shown in the letter of hypothecation;
2 that no lien exists on the goods apart from any resulting from warehousing, port charges or freight which may be due but unpaid;
3 that insurance is in existence, for an adequate amount, on the goods and will be maintained throughout the period of the pledge; and
4 that any mistake in the description of the goods as shown in the documents will adversely affect the rights of the bank. While it is beyond the scope of this book to comment on the legal considerations underlying the pledge of goods, these are important and banks will investigate with great care the documents deposited.

If the bank has possession of the goods warehoused in its name, how then can the importer arrange sale in order to acquire funds to repay the bank? A reasonable question which frequently arises in practice. The answer is that banks will agree to release goods to undoubted customers 'in trust' for that particular purpose against signature of a trust receipt. This document undertakes that the borrower will hold the goods in trust for the bank and furthermore that in the event of sale the proceeds will be similarly held and paid to the bank in repayment or reduction of the loan. Under the agreement the borrower must store the goods in such a way that they are readily identifiable from other goods and must maintain adequate insurance.

11

Other Trading Methods

To complete our examination of the financial aspects of exporting it is necessary to consider briefly those relating to a number of specialized methods of trading:

1 consignment trading;
2 joint ventures overseas;
3 pick-a-back schemes and group selling;
4 royalty agreements; and
5 licensing.

The descriptions of each method which follow are summaries only sufficient to explain the financial implications and readers are advised to read the companion book in this series, *Principles of International Marketing*, for details of these channels of distribution and their significance in ensuring that the most profitable commercial marketing strategy is adopted.

Consignment Trading

The normal direct export is from the seller either to an agent or distributor who is on-selling or to an end user (direct buyer). Settlement is made by the agent or distributor or direct buyer to the exporter, with or without a credit period, in accordance with the method of payment agreed between them. There may however be marketing benefits in allowing an agent or distributor to hold stocks of goods for which no immediate orders are in existence but for which there is a buoyant demand and, in consequence, an advantage in having items constantly available for either supply at short notice or inspection.

Where goods are supplied to an importer, normally an agent, on this basis the description is 'consignment trading' and the importer is subject to all the customary duties to safeguard the goods as agent of the exporter who remains the owner. *Principles of Law relating to Overseas Trade*, another companion book in this series, sets out the legal responsibilities in detail. The range of goods suitable for consignment trading is also limited as *Principles of International Marketing* will indicate.

From the financial viewpoint, consignment trading introduces an element of uncertainty about time in the payment arrangements. It is unlikely that the importer will be in a position to give more than an informed estimate of the speed at which sales of the 'consigned' goods will take place, and even if this is reasonably accurate there is always the unforeseeable hitch. Thus exporters must consider carefully the amount of consigned goods which they can afford to finance without damage to cash flow. Financial dangers also lurk in the commercial morality of both the market and the importer. The need for checks on both country and buyer risks are equally if not more important where consignment trading is contemplated; the knowledge that legal possession remains in the hands of the exporter may be small consolation if retrieval involves delay, expense and even litigation – any one of which could spell disaster to the small exporter.

A degree of protection may be obtainable by seeking credit insurance which is available for stocks held overseas, and in some cases the importer may be prepared to agree to pay a percentage of the value of consignment stocks on receipt (with the balance payable when on-sales are completed) which is a help to the exporter's cash flow. The practice of consignment trading has received some impetus in recent years through the establishment in various markets of free ports or customs free areas where imported goods may be held without payment of import duties until sales take place, at which time the duty becomes payable. This system obviously decreases the financial burden of holding stocks under a consignment arrangement.

Joint Ventures Overseas

In chapter 1 we analysed the practice of direct investment abroad by companies, particularly multinationals, seeking to expand their trading beyond the confines of direct exporting or to discover alternative methods of trade when direct exporting is no longer viable. One of the methods then identified was the joint venture whereby the exporter and a local company in the market concerned jointly contributed to a new venture designed to increase penetration of the market, often by the exporter investing through the remittance of funds, supply of capital equipment or goods for assembly. However the term 'joint venture' is equally applicable to an arrangement between exporter and buyer to undertake jointly the expenses of a transaction (or series of transactions) and to share in agreed percentages the profits arising. This might for example be a favourable method of exploiting a temporary situation creating a trade opportunity not normally arising, by forming a basis for the sharing of expenses and profits in circumstances where a mutual interest exists.

Pick-a-Back Schemes and Group Selling

One of the difficulties facing a small firm wishing to enter export markets is the time and expense necessary firstly to research the suitability and demand for its products overseas and secondly to set up effective marketing facilities, for example the selection of suitable agents and the conclusion of satisfactory agreements. Government encouragement has been given on several occasions to schemes, known as pick-a-back, intended to assist through large companies offering their research facilities to smaller firms usually producing complementary and not competing products, and allowing them to use the large company's existing agency network in international markets.

This need not affect the payment for the goods which usually comes direct to the new exporter, although it might in some instances be received via the large company. Where there are considerable financial benefits is in the reliability of the agent network which is probably well-tested and monitored by the present user, and the considerable expertise through the research department which might well save the new exporter from costly mistakes in approaching inappropriate markets.

Although it might be inferred from the above that this is a beneficial course for a new exporter to adopt, one must add that the number of successful schemes launched appears to have been very limited. It is also apparent that negotiations intended to create a pick-a-back scheme can result in the small firm being offered an opportunity to become voluntarily a subsidiary of the larger firm or indeed be taken over. As no statistics are available and it is quite possible many small firms do have informal arrangements with established exporters, it is impos-sible to evaluate the merits of possible future initiatives in this field despite the seeming attractiveness of the theory.

Group selling consists of the setting up by groups of joint marketing arrangements including among others: research advertising, showrooms, shipping and sales staff. In some instances finance is also arranged on a group basis. The object is the achievement of efficient administration at minimum cost to maximize the potential for members' products. It has to be said once again, with regret, that there is little published evidence of the success of group selling except in the case of one or two groups such as pottery, where the structure of the industry and product range appear particularly suited to the concept.

Royalty Agreements and Licensing

The difficulties of penetrating a market may result from a variety of factors. Less developed countries frequently adopt a policy in relation to imports which is restrictive and aimed at promoting and subsequently nurturing infant industries, to encourage employment prospects and achieve independence. State controlled economies may display similar characteristics but with the object of promoting industries which are able to satisfy speedily a public outcry for consumer goods. In both cases there is a tremendous demand for knowhow to further local industries' growth, although imports for certain goods may be frustrated and this knowhow provides opportunities for United Kingdom suppliers. The knowhow may be sold to a local firm enabling it to manufacture products and, in addition to the purchase price, royalties will be paid at an agreed rate on the products sold. Alternatively the United Kingdom manufacturer may license an overseas company to manufacture products, sometimes using the manufacturer's brand name, with royalties similarly payable on sales.

Postscript

In the research necessary to produce a book designed to offer simple assistance to exporters wrestling with the financial problems of securing payment and advice, one must encounter the feelings these exporters have towards the financial services industry in general and banking in particular.

Banking is currently undergoing considerable change forced upon it by the effects of recession and the need to reinforce its essential reputation for stability, evidenced by strong balance sheets, on which its future both domestically and internationally depends. Many of the cost containment measures, including branch closures and staff reductions, have caused an unavoidable degree of inconvenience to their customers and are inevitably portrayed by some as indicating a declining standard of service. There is also a widely voiced apprehension that banks may lose the ability, willingness or time to devote the attention necessary to understand the individual problems of their customers and to offer advice. Great reliance has been placed in the past on these qualities which have formed a basic element in building strong bank-customer relations, in a phrase, 'the personal touch'.

In this context measures which will assist in an improvement in the image of banks include those intended to heighten the perception among corporate managers and branch staff of financial problems as seen by their customers in their everyday trading. Nowhere is this more relevant than in the case of companies exporting or seeking to export. This book attempts to survey financial questions through the eyes of the exporter not those of the bank. It is not intended to be a banking textbook but it is commended to bankers and customers alike as a contribution towards mutual understanding and in consequence, a strengthening of the trust and respect which have been the traditional cornerstones of a successful account relationship.

Questions for Discussion

Chapter 1

1 What is the law of comparative costs?

2 How have economic and political changes since World War II affected the pattern of international trade?

3 How has international debt affected Lesser Developed Countries and what part has countertrade played in this situation?

4 What are the advantages and risks involved in direct investment overseas?

5 Why is GATT important in facilitating world trade?

6 What is the history of the European Community from its inception to the present day?

Chapter 2

1 What is country risk and how can it be evaluated?

2 Why are the activities of the International Monetary Fund and the World Bank of assistance to exporters?

3 How can buyer risk be minimized?

4 What is the purpose of credit insurance and how does it operate?

Chapter 3

1 Are you able to list costs comprised in the basic price of goods and those to be added under various delivery terms?

2 Sellers' and buyers' interests are diametrically opposed at the outset of negotiations for an export sale. Can you quote examples?

3 What are the main factors influencing competition in export markets?

4 How do export merchants and confirming houses operate?

Chapter 4

1 What are 'spot' and 'forward' foreign exchange rates and how are they quoted?

2 What is 'exchange risk' and how does it arise?

3 How does a forward exchange contract operate?

4 In what circumstances are pure currency options particularly valuable to exporters?

5 Can nations, through collective action, mitigate the effects of exchange rate movements on trade?

6 What is the European Currency Unit (ECU) and its uses?

7 What are the origins and history of the Exchange Rate Mechanism?

8 Are there methods of avoiding exchange risk and cost which are particularly appropriate to the importing and exporting company?

Chapter 5

1 By what criteria should an exporter's suggestion as to method of payment be assessed?

2 How many common financial causes for loss in export transactions can you list?

3 Explain the role of a credit controller and its importance.

4 How many different methods of payment exist and can you describe them?

5 How would you endeavour to achieve settlement under an export on open account?

Chapter 6

1 What is a bill of exchange? Draw up a specimen.

2 How can both seller and buyer obtain security under a documentary collection method of payment?

3 What is the meaning of 'protesting' a bill of exchange?

4 Could you explain the significance of questions asked on a bank's documents for collection form?

5 Can you quote examples of clauses commonly used on bills of exchange? What are the 'Uniform Rules for Collection'?

Chapter 7

1 What differentiates a letter of credit from other methods of payment?

2 Who are the parties to a documentary credit?

3 Define a revocable, an irrevocable and an irrevocable confirmed letter of credit – when should each be suggested to a buyer?

4 Transferable, revolving and red clause are types of letter of credit. Can you describe the characteristics and purpose of each?

5 Who bears the costs of a letter of credit?

Chapter 8

1 How should the examination of a letter of credit on receipt be conducted by the beneficiary to ensure its terms are acceptable?

2 What is the doctrine of strict compliance?

3 In what manner should the examination of documents against the terms of a letter of credit be carried out prior to presentation to the bank?

4 What remedies exist to the exporter if documents are rejected when presented under a letter of credit?

Chapter 9

1 Why are firms inviting tenders at risk in respect of responses?

2 What risks are experienced by a buyer when contracting with a successful tenderer?

3 How do banker's guarantees help to minimize these risks?

4 What should an exporter consider when asking his bank to issue tender, performance or advance payment guarantees?

Chapter 10

1 When seeking bank finance in establishing export markets what information should be presented to the bank?

2 What information do banks require when asked to provide contract (or shipment) to settlement finance?

3 How can credit insurance assist in obtaining export finance?

4 What part do bills of exchange play in obtaining export finance?

5 How can factoring and forfaiting assist an exporter?

6 Is the importer able to obtain finance against the goods and, if so, how?

Chapter 11

1 What is meant by 'consignment trading'?

2 Several schemes have been tried to enable firms to co-operate in export selling; can you describe them?

3 What part do royalty agreements and licensing play in exporting?

Topics Which Can Form the Basis for a Company Seminar

Chapter 1

What stage in development have we reached in our exporting to individual markets? Is there potential for further expansion in each market and, if so, how should this be exploited?

Chapter 2

How does our company endeavour to limit both country and buyer risks in each of our markets and could we do more?

Chapter 3

The art, or skill, behind our quoting – what are the factors included in the quote and how are they to be evaluated?

Chapter 4

What has been our company's experience in foreign currency as contrasted with sterling quoting, and how has it determined our current policy on minimizing exchange risk?

Chapter 5

What do we consider the role of a credit controller to be and how can we achieve the constant liaison between all disciplines involved in an export transaction necessary to ensure the success of that role?

Chapter 8

What determines our policy in deciding when to ask for a letter of credit? Do we pay or contribute towards costs? What is our track record in securing payment on first presentation? What did it cost us in interest payable or lost in those cases where documents were refused? Are our examination procedures on receipt of a credit and prior to the presentation of documents effective?

Chapter 9

When does our type of business justify the buyer requesting bank guarantees? What is our risk and liability if we agree?

Chapter 10

How does our company finance its exports and what contribution can we all make to improve cash flow and render finance arrangements trouble free?

Index